Law School Survival Guide

BUSINESS ORGANIZATIONS

Outlines and Case Summaries

t TellerBooks

BUSINESS ORGANIZATIONS:
Outlines and Case Studies™

Law School Survival Guides

JuraLaw

Published by JURALAW™
an imprint of TELLERBOOKS™

tellerbooks.com/juralaw
contact@tellerbooks.com

ISBN (13) (paperback): 978-1-68109-056-6
ISBN (10) (paperback): 1-68109-056-2
ISBN (13) (Kindle): 978-1-68109-057-3
ISBN (10) (Kindle): 1-68109-057-0
ISBN (13) (ePub): 978-1-68109-058-0
ISBN (10) (ePub): 1-68109-058-9

2016 Edition
Manufactured in the U.S.A.

DISCLAIMER: Although this book is designed to provide rigorously researched information, it is intended not as a definitive statement of the law, but rather, as a concise and general overview that will help readers to understand basic legal principles and find further information, if necessary. Because the law changes rapidly through new statutes and innovative judicial decisions, law books, including this one, may quickly become outdated. Furthermore, some decisions may be ambiguous and subject to differing interpretations and other sources may come to conclusions distinct from those presented herein. Nothing in this book forms an attorney-client relationship or is intended to constitute legal advice, which should be obtained through consultation with a qualified attorney.

ABBREVIATED CONTENTS

Appendices

TABLE OF CONTENTS

Appendices

ABBREVIATIONS

BVI company .... British Virgin Islands company
Exchange Act............... Securities Exchange Act of 1934
IPO............................. Initial public offering
IRC............................. Internal Revenue Code
L Corp .... Used in the examples presented to represent a fictitious large corporation
Lat.............................. Latin
LLC .... Limited Liability Company
LLP............................. Limited Liability Partnership
LP............................... Limited Partnership
MBCA .... Model Business Corporation Act
NASD.......................... National Association of Securities Dealers
NASDAQ..................... National Association of Securities Dealers Automated Quotations
NYSE .... New York Stock Exchange
RLA............................. Restatement of the Law (Second) of Agency
RUPA.......................... Revised Uniform Partnership Act (of 1994 or 1997)
S Corp[1] .... Used in the examples presented to represent a fictitious small corporation
S. Ct........................... Supreme Court
SEC............................ Securities and Exchange Commission
Securities Act............... The Securities Act of 1933
SLC .... Special Litigation Committee
ULLCA .... Uniform Limited Liability Company Act
UPA............................ Uniform Partnership Act of 1914
USC .... United States Code

---

[1] The abbreviation "S Corp" should not be confused with the "S corporation," a type of tax-exempt corporation. To avoid confusion, "S corporation" will always be fully written out.

Part I: Introduction and General Principles

1 Introduction

1.1 The Business Organization: an Overview

1.1.1 Definition

(a)   A business organization is a legal entity through which investors and entrepreneurs provide goods and services and engage in trade and other wealth-generating activities. Traditionally, the menu of American business organizations was comprised of the general partnership and the corporation. Other entities, such as limited liability companies and limited liability partnerships, are in many ways hybrids or statutorily-created variations of partnerships or corporations.

(b)   Although a company may appear to be one business association, it may in reality prove to be a multi-tiered conglomerate comprised of many corporations, partnerships and other business entities. This is in fact the case of many large corporations and other organizations. In order to circumvent limitations as to the kinds of activities they may undertake, many such companies are organized with very general corporate charters whose language is articulated such that they may engage in "any lawful activity," thus allowing them to serve as umbrella organizations of a large and diverse set of subsidiary companies.

1.1.2 The Variety of Business Organizations

(a)   Traditionally, there has been a tension between entrepreneurs, who have long sought to expand the menu of business forms available and governments, which have resisted such efforts by limiting the available menu. In the United States, the entrepreneur nonetheless has a wide variety of business organizations from which to choose, from small, closely held firms to large, public corporations.

(b)   The management practices of business organizations can be as diverse as the forms that business organizations can take. While in small firms, owners and managers are generally the same group of people, in large organizations, a large number of generally passive stockholders which is distinct from the managers usually owns the company.[2] Thus, in small firms, where a small number of managers own the business, decisions are usually made by consensus. In large organizations, in contrast, there may be tens of thousands of shareholders, thus rendering decisions by consensus impractical. In these organizations, policy is generally developed through majority voting.

(c)   As a final point of contrast, whereas small firms are usually run informally and without a hierarchy, large organizations are run under a formal set of rules establishing tiers of control and duties among shareholders, directors and officers. The relationships among these actors will be explored later on in the chapters that follow.

1.2 Factors to Consider When Choosing a Business Entity

1.2.1 General Overview

(a)   Any individuals who form a business must agree on such fundamental issues as control, ownership and dissolution of the business. When the individuals choose a specific entity through which to conduct the activity, many of these questions are automatically determined through the

---

[2] The managers may, however, as part of their compensation, own some level of stock in the company.

11

respective entity's legally-prescribed default settings. The individuals forming the company may then contract around or customize the default settings in order to suit their business needs, as long as the new rules conform to public policy considerations. A clause whose content violates such policy considerations (*e.g.*, one denying the right of third parties to make claims against the reckless conduct of the owners) would be held null and void in the relevant jurisdiction and the default rules would spring into application.

1.2.2 Factors

Before choosing a business entity, the goals of the business owners should be assessed in light of the following factors:

(a)   Tax Treatment

The form that a business association takes will have a significant impact on the tax treatment that it receives. The law taxes some business organizations, exempts others fully and offers a gray area for many others in between. Some associations that fall into this gray area include those that are exempted from taxes up until they reach a certain size or profit margin. When they reach such dimensions, they are taxed as ordinary incorporated entities. When this occurs, double taxation applies, since, in addition to the business organization, the dividends of the owners are also taxed. For example, if the business owners form a C corporation, taxation will apply to both the shareholders' dividends as well as to the corporation's profits. If, however, the owners opt for an S corporation, pass-through taxation will occur, with taxation applied only to the shareholders' dividends (the corporation itself will not be recognized under the law as a legal person and thus will not be subject to taxation). In addition to S corporations, limited liability companies and partnerships are subject to pass-through taxation. All of these organizations are "invisible" under the tax code, which taxes only the salaries or dividends of the respective partners or shareholders.

(b)   Owners' Liability

The way that a business is organized affects the extent to which its owners could be held liable for the business's debts. Some organizations, such as the corporation, shield their managers from company debt whenever the managers exercise business judgment and reasonable investigation. In other organizations, the owners, managers or partners are held personally, jointly and severally liable for the debts of the enterprise, regardless of the extent to which business judgment was exercised. The incorporation of a business thus offers entrepreneurs a valuable protection that permits them to undertake activities that might otherwise prove to be too risky.

(c)   Governance

Governance deals with the question of whom is given the right to participate in the management and decision making of a business. The rules of governance are substantially determined by the form that the owners of a company choose and these rules vary substantially among partnerships and corporations, with limited liability companies offering a regime that blends elements of both the corporate and partnership model. Governance may also influence whether the owners are directly responsible for the governance of the organization or whether they govern through others that they have selected. For example, in public corporations, the owners govern through their elected directors, who in turn select the corporation's officers (the president, treasurer, etc.). In contrast, the owners of a closely held corporation are directly responsible for the company's governance.

(d)　　Raising Capital

Yet another factor that the choice of entity affects is the extent of options available for entrepreneurs to raise funds for their business. Some organizations require business owners to raise capital directly with their own funds or through loans, while others permit them to raise funds indirectly by, for example, issuing shares of stock. The amount of funds needed to start a business may thus influence the choice of entity. For example, when modest start-up capital is needed, the owners may opt for a limited liability company, but when they must raise more substantial sums, they may form a corporation, which allows for outside investors to purchase company equity in the form of stock.

(e)　　Exit Strategies

Finally, business owners should consider the available exit strategies of their chosen business entity. In some organizations, such as the S corporation, the exit strategy is relatively cumbersome, since there is no ready market to sell shares of equity. In others, such as the public corporation, exiting is far simpler and consists of selling shares of stock on the public market.

2   Agency

2.1   Defining Agency

Agency can be defined as the fiduciary relation that results from the manifestation of: (i) consent by one person to another that the other will act on his behalf and subject to his control; and (ii) consent by the other to so act.[3] The agent owes a fiduciary duty to a second party, known as the principal, who consents to the agent's acting on his behalf. The agent has the power to alter the legal obligations and rights of the principal, who may be bound by or held liable for the acts or omissions of the agent.

A principal is a person who designates an agent to undertake an action on the principal's behalf. Once the principal designates an agent, the agency relationship begins. For example, in *Gorton v. Doty* (Idaho Ct. App. 1937), the plaintiff sued the owner of a vehicle that had been involved in a traffic accident that injured the plaintiff. The owner was not driving the vehicle at the time that the plaintiff was injured. Therefore, he was not directly liable. The court nevertheless found the owner liable for injuring the plaintiff, since he lent the vehicle to a third party, designated the third party and requested that only he drive. The court concluded that an express condition precedent was created for the owner's lending of the car, a condition that was accepted by the third party. Furthermore, there is a presumption that the owner of the car is the principal of a driver borrowing the car. An agency relationship was therefore created and the defendant owner was liable.

The dissent argued the possibility that the defendant's request (that only the third party drive) was *not* a favor that she (the owner) was asking that conferred a benefit to her (the owner). Rather, the request was that the law be respected; she did not want some teenage member of the sports league illegally driving the car. Since no evidence showed that the defendant ordered or commanded the third party to take the car, the dissent argued that no agency relationship was established.

One factor that can be looked to when determining whether an agency relationship exists is control. When a third party has control, an agency relationship usually exists. For example, a debtor can be held to be the agent of a creditor if the creditor becomes sufficiently involved in the control of the debtor's day-to-day operations.

> For example, in *Gay Jenson Farms Co. v. Cargill, Inc.* (Minn. 1981), the plaintiffs sued a defendant debtor and a defendant creditor for funds lost when the debtor defaulted on contracts. The defendant creditor was held to have been a principal of the debtor because it was actively involved in the debtor's operations by making recommendations, requiring approval before the debtor entered into mortgages and making economic decisions. The creditor was therefore held liable for the debts.

2.2   Liability of Principals to Third Parties in Tort

2.2.1   Servant versus Independent Contractor

(a)   The words used in a contract describing the relationship between an owner and operator are not dispositive in determining whether agency exists. The most important factor that courts consider is the degree of control of an owner over a company. The more control exercised over a company and its operator, the more likely it is that an agency relationship exists.

---

[3] RLA § 1.

(b)   Thus, a principal cannot escape liability for an operator's torts just because the operator is referred to as an "independent contractor" in the contract. The owner can be held liable to a third party for the operator's negligence. In *Humble Oil & Refining Co. v. Martin* (Tex. 1949), the plaintiff was injured by a car rolling out of a service station run by the operating defendant. Although the operating defendant was referred to as a "contractor" in the contract with the defendant owner, an agency relationship was held to exist because the owner exercised much control over the day to day operations of the company. He paid some of the operating defendant's expenses, set store hours and played a role in decision making.

(c)   This rule applies even where a franchisor/franchisee relationship exists. As defined in *Murphy v. Holiday Inns, Inc.* (Va. 1975), a franchise is a system for selective distribution of goods or services under a brand name through outlets owned by independent businessmen called "franchisees." When the franchisor exercises sufficient control over the franchisee's activities, an agency relationship arises. In *Miller v. McDonald's Corp.* (Or. App. 1997), for example, the plaintiff injured her tooth when biting into a hamburger and sued the defendant franchisor. Summary judgment for the franchisor was reversed when the court held that there was enough evidence to establish agency—the franchisor maintained a *right to exercise control* over the franchisee's operations. The franchisor was therefore liable for the franchisee restaurant's negligence.

(d)   In *Hoover v. Sun Oil Co.* (Del. 1965), on the other hand, an agency relationship was not found. Here, the plaintiff sued a service station franchisor and operator when he was injured by a fire at the station. The court held that the defendant franchisor did not exercise sufficient control over the franchisee's operations to create an agency relationship and was thus not liable for the franchisee's negligence. Rather, the franchisee was treated as an independent contractor, setting its own decisions and policies, such as store hours and cleanliness. Although Sun Oil Co. products were being sold, this was insufficient to establish an agency relationship.

2.2.2   Liability for Torts of Independent Contractors

Generally speaking, no agency relationship arises for acts of independent contractors. However, certain exceptions apply, including the following:

(a)   When a landowner retains control of the manner in which the independent contractor does the work;

(b)   When the independent contractor is incompetent;

(c)   When there is a nuisance—an abnormally dangerous activity.

Majestic Realty Associates, Inc. v. Toti Contracting Co. (N.J. 1959) clearly demonstrates this third scenario. In *Majestic Realty*, the defendant was contracted by the City of Paterson to demolish a building. While doing so, the defendant damaged the plaintiff's building. The plaintiff sued the City of Paterson on an agency theory that argued that the City was the defendant's principal. The City argued that the defendant was an independent contractor and that the City should not be held liable. The court held that, although a contractor normally is not liable for the negligence of its independent contractors, here, the City is liable because the defendant was involved in a nuisance/inherently dangerous activity: the demolishing of a building on a busy street.

2.2.3   Scope of Employment

(a) In order for a principal to be liable for his agent's acts, the agent must be acting within the scope of his employment. Formerly, this meant that the employee must have been working in furtherance of the purposes of the principal. However, a more flexible definition has been recently used by the courts in determining when an agent acts within the scope of employment. Such courts include any acts taken while the agent is engaged in *any foreseeable activity* while he is furthering the purposes of the principal, regardless of whether this activity actually served the purposes of the employer.

(b) A federal court in *Ira S. Bushey & Sons, Inc. v. United States* (2d Cir. 1968) took an especially liberal approach to this question. In Bushey, a seaman working for the defendant United States returned to his ship drunk and opened valves that caused the boat to sink, damaging the plaintiff's drydock. Although the seaman, an agent of the United States, was in no way acting to further the purposes of the United States, his employer, the employer was nevertheless held liable, since it was foreseeable that a seaman would get drunk and cause such an incident. The court held that the employee was thus within his scope of employment.[4]

(c) If a plaintiff wishes to hold a defendant liable for the acts of an employee, the plaintiff has the burden of proving that the defendant's employee was acting within the scope of his employment. This can sometimes lead to unexpected results. For example, in *Manning v. Grimsley* (1st Cir.1981), the plaintiff sued the defendant baseball player and his employer when the defendant threw a baseball at and injured him, after the plaintiff heckled him. The court reasoned that if evidence is presented showing that the defendant threw the ball at the plaintiff as a reaction to the heckler's present interference of his ability to perform, then his employer could be held liable. If, however, it was not directly provoked by the heckler, then the employer would not be liable because the defendant's act, unprovoked, would have been unforeseeable and outside of the scope of his employment. Here, sufficient evidence was presented showing that the defendant threw the ball at the plaintiff in reaction to the plaintiff's provoking him. For example, the defendant looked at the hecklers, not just at the stands.

2.2.4 Statutory Claims

(a) Before a defendant can be sued for the tort of a third party, the plaintiff must prove that an agency relationship between the defendant and the third party exists. To do this, the plaintiff must show that the defendant-principal consented in allowing the agent to act on his behalf and that the agent agreed to act on the defendant-principal's behalf.

(b) In *Arguello v. Conoco, Inc.* (5th Cir. 2000), minority groups sued the defendant for the discriminatory practices of the defendant's stores that allegedly violated federal law. The court held that no agency relationship existed between the defendant and the Conoco-branded stores, since the agreements that allowed the branded stores to sell Conoco gasoline expressly stated that the stores were independent businesses with no agency relationship. However, because the employees of the Conoco-owned stores acted as agents of the defendant when discriminating, an agency relationship exists. The court ruled in favor of the plaintiffs with respect to the Conoco-owned stores.

---

[4] It should be noted that this case seems to contradict § 228 (c) of the Restatement of the Law of Agency, which requires some purpose of the employer to be promoted. It is possible that the judge arrived at this reading of agency law in order to reach a desired result, *i.e.*, the United States, with its deep pockets, reimburse the dry-dock owner.

2.3 Liability of Principals to Third Parties in Contract

A principal may empower an employee to act on his behalf by granting him authority that may be actual, apparent, express or implied. Furthermore, some relationships give an employee inherent agency power without any explicit act by the principal.

2.3.1 Actual Authority

(a) Actual authority may be express or implied. A principal gives an agent actual express authority when he explicitly tells the agent to take a certain action. If a principal commands an agent to enter into a contract with a third party, for example and the agent does so, the principal is bound by the contract. The third party can enforce the contract against the principal, even if he did not realize at the time that the agent was acting on behalf of the principal.

(b) Actual authority can also be implied. A principal cannot always think of everything that it would authorize his agent to do. If, in order to carry out the principal's explicit instructions, the agent takes some necessary steps, the principal is bound by the agent's actions. The principal therefore has an incentive to draft good instructions. If the principal does not provide detailed instructions as to how the agent should achieve a particular task, then the principal is bound by whatever the agent does if he carries out the instruction in a normal manner.

(c) Thus, if an employer leaves questions open for an employee without drafting specific terms and negligence results from the employee's decisions, the employer is liable. Of course, this only applies if an agency relationship already exists. If, however, the employee is an independent contractor, the general rule where employers are not bound by the contractors' acts would apply. If an employer leaves open instructions for an independent contractor who acts negligently, the principal is not liable.

(d) When an agent is required to hire an employee in order to complete the work assigned to him by a principal, the hiring is permitted within the agent's authority. In *Mill Street Church of Christ v. Sam Hogan* (Ky. Ct. App.), for example, the defendant church hired Bill Hogan to paint the church, who then hired his brother, the plaintiff, to aid him. The plaintiff was injured on the job and was awarded compensation, since Bill Hogan had implied authority to hire him. The defendant church challenged this ruling, but the decision for the plaintiff was affirmed because Bill Hogan had authority to hire his brother, since (i) he could not do the work by himself and therefore had implied authority; and (ii) he had apparent authority, since from the plaintiff's perspective, it is reasonable that brother, who hired him in the past, would hire him again. The church, through its actions, implicitly ratified Sam Hogan's painting of the church.

2.3.2 Apparent Authority

(a) Even when an agent lacks express or implied actual authority, there are situations in which an agent may bind a principal. One such situation involves apparent authority, which applies when the principal represents to a third party that the agent is authorized to enter into a contract. The key to apparent authority is that *the principal must make a representation.*

(b) The third party must reasonably believe that the agent has the authority to act on behalf of the principal. If it is not reasonable, the principal will not be bound. The reasonableness test is taken from the third party's perspective. The court is to determine what a reasonable third party would believe. In *Lind v. Schenley Industries, Inc.* (3d Cir. 1960), the plaintiff's supervisor offered him a promotion that would have significantly increased his salary. After working several years without receiving the increased salary, the plaintiff sued to recover. The defendant employer argued that because the plaintiff's supervisor did not have authority to grant the raise, the employer was not bound to deliver it. The court held for the plaintiff, holding that the plaintiff had every reason to believe that his supervisor was an agent authorized to offer the salary increase. Also, since the vice president told the plaintiff that he would be promoted and that his supervisor would tell him his new salary, the plaintiff was reasonable in believing that his supervisor did indeed have such authority.

(c)   In an employer-employee relationship, an agency relationship exists that binds an employer to his employee's sales, even when the employer did not agree to a sale, when the sale is reasonable. Apparent authority is imparted upon the employee as soon as he is hired. In *Three-Seventy Leasing Corporation v. Amex Corporation* (5th Cir. 1976), the defendant's salesperson entered into a contract to sell computers to the plaintiff even though the defendant did not give him authority to do so. The defendant later reneged on the contract because of the plaintiff's credit. When the plaintiff sued for breach of contract, the court enforced the contract because it was reasonable for the plaintiff to assume that the salesperson was authorized by the defendant to enter into the transaction. If the sale was not reasonable given the nature of the business, the salesperson would not have been given such authority. For example, a car dealership employee's agreement to purchase a dozen washing machines probably would not be binding on the car dealership, since it would be unreasonable to assume that a car dealership would give an employee such authority to make such as purchase.

2.3.3   Inherent Agency Power

(a)   For many lawyers and commentators, the idea of inherent agency power makes little sense. It is often invoked by courts when they want to protect a third party, but there is no actual authority or insufficient manifestations by the principal to the third party to justify apparent authority. In such cases, courts commit the principal to acts of the agent that, while not authorized, are very close to that which agents are normally authorized to do.

(b)   Inherent agency power allows an agent to enter into binding contracts with third parties even when the details of those contracts exceed the authority given to the agent. The main question that inherent agency questions pose is whether the decisions taken by the agent would *usually* be within his decision-making power. This rule holds true even when there are specific instructions given to the agent telling him that he is unauthorized to make such provisions, provided that such instructions are not made known to the third party.

(c)   In *Watteau v. Fenwick* (Queen's Bench 1892), the defendant business owner granted Humble authority to make purchases, an authority that Humble exceeded. The court held for the plaintiff, who sued to enforce the contract. The court reasoned that making the purchases was within Humble's inherent agency power. Principals are bound by all decisions usually within the authority of their agents, even if the principal specifically instructed the agent not to take the actions in question.

(d)   When an agent makes decisions that are necessary in order for him to achieve his assigned tasks, the principal is bound by the decisions, even if the agent was not specifically authorized to make them. Consider, for example, *Kid v. Thomas A. Edison, Inc.* (S.D.N.Y. 1917), where the principal was bound by the agent's promise to pay recital fees, even though the principal never authorized the agent to make such decisions. See also *Nogales Service Center v. Atlantic Richfield Co.* (Ariz. 1980), where the plaintiff argued that the defendant's agent had set a certain pricing policy with the plaintiff. When the defendant refused to honor the policy, the plaintiff sued. The court held that even if an agent lacks express and apparent authority to make decisions, the principal can still be bound by the agent's decisions when those decisions fall within the incidental, inherent powers authorized by the agent's post.[5]

2.3.4 Ratification

(a) Ratification applies in cases where an agent enters into a contract, even though he had no express or implied authority to do so. When the agent lacks inherent agency power, the principal is generally not bound by the agent's decisions.

(b) This is where the concept of ratification applies. If the principal ratifies the agreement, it becomes as though the agent had authority to enter into the contract. Once the plaintiff adopts contract, it becomes binding. However, if the plaintiff, upon hearing about the unauthorized contract, objects to it, he is no longer bound.

(c) Absent actual or apparent authority, inherent agency power or ratification, an individual is not bound by an unauthorized person's representations on behalf of the individual. For example, if a person enters into an unauthorized contract on behalf of an individual who does not ratify the contract, the individual is not bound by the unauthorized contract or by the representations to a third party. For example, in *Botticello v. Stefanovicz* (Conn. 1979), defendants Walter and Mary Stefanovicz were tenants in common on a piece of property. Walter, without the permission of Mary, offered the plaintiff an options agreement to buy the property. The plaintiff apparently had not done a title search and was unaware that the title was held as a tenancy in common. Furthermore, Walter Stefanovicz did not tell the plaintiff that his wife was a tenant in common. Walter later failed to honor the options agreement and the plaintiff sued for specific performance. He argued that there was an agency relationship between Walter and Mary through marriage and that Walter therefore had authority to offer the option. The court rejected this reasoning, holding that marriage on its own does not create agency. The issue it considers is whether a person is bound to a third party when a second person makes unauthorized representations. The court answered in the negative: an individual is not bound by representations made by an unauthorized party to a third party, unless he ratifies the agreement. Here, since Mary did not ratify the agreement, the contract was not enforceable. The judgment was given to the defendant. This case shows that "implicit ratification" is not recognized by the courts. The plaintiff's argument that Mary had ratified the agreement by knowing about it and accepting the money was rejected because she never explicitly signed or ratified the agreement.

2.3.5 Estoppel

(a) Agency may be created by estoppel if an individual represents himself to be an authorized agent. Agency by estoppel may arise even when the alleged principal does nothing to represent that the individual is in fact an authorized agent. In such cases, courts consider whether the alleged principal either manifested that the alleged agent was authorized or was negligent in doing nothing to stop the alleged agent from deceiving the third party.

(b) The mere representation of a charlatan agent on its own is not enough to establish agency. The principal must contribute to the misrepresentation by either an act or a negligent omission. In *Hoddeson v. Koos Bros..* (N.J. Super. App. Div. 1957), for example, a con artist represented to the plaintiff that he was the defendant furniture store's salesman, sold her furniture and then left with her money. When the furniture was not delivered, the plaintiff sued the defendant, alleging an agency relationship between the defendant and the third party. Although the trial court found an agency relationship, the appeals court did not, holding that the plaintiff must show that the

---

[5] Note, however, that in this case, the court gave judgment to the defendant, only because of the plaintiff's evidentiary mistake.

defendant *did something* to project either express, implied or apparent authority to the con artist. The defendant did no such thing. The court went on to state that this rule was unjust in modern department stores and allowed the plaintiff to recover if she could show that the defendant was negligent in allowing the con artist to sell the furniture. Under such a showing, agency by estoppel will be established. A new trial was allowed with the opportunity for the plaintiff to present such evidence.

2.3.6 Agent's Liability on the Contract

(a) In order for an agent to avoid personal liability on a contract, he must disclose to the principal that he is acting on behalf of a principal. He must also disclose the identity of the principal. In *Atlantic Salmon A/S v. Curran* (Mass. App. Ct. 1992), the defendant, who partially disclosed that he was a representative of the principal, made representations that he would purchase the plaintiff's salmon. He then never purchased the salmon. The plaintiff sued for specific performance. The defendant argued that he was merely an agent. The trial court agreed and granted judgment to him, holding that he was simply acting as an agent for Boston International Seafood Exchange, Inc. The appeals court reversed, since Boston International Seafood Exchange was merely a shell organization of Marketing Designs, Inc. and the defendant represented only that he was an agent of Boston International, not Marketing Designs, Inc. Since he never disclosed the true identity of the principal, he was held personally liable for the amount in controversy.

(b) An agent is not liable if he fully discloses the full name of the person for whom he is contracting. In *Atlantic Salmon*, however, this was not the case. Since he only partially disclosed the principal's identity, the court held that he was contracting not in his principal's name, but rather, in his own name. Since he contracted personally, he was personally liable. Otherwise, it is presumed that the agent intended to be a party to the contract when the principal's identity is only partially disclosed. Restatement (Second) of Agency, § 321.

(c) The partial disclosure of the identity of one's principal is insufficient in protecting an agent from personal liability. The third party must know exactly who the principal is or the agent is liable. This helps third parties to evaluate the reputation of the principal and other factors that are important to consider before entering into a contract.

2.4 Fiduciary Obligations of Agents

2.4.1 Duties during Agency

An agent's primary duty is to protect and serve the interests of his principal. It is a duty of loyalty. He is forbidden from accepting any outside compensation in relation to the agency unless the principal is aware of and approves the compensation. Consider the following examples:

(a) A purchases land for $125,000 and sells it to B for $200,000. A never tells B how much she paid for it. B has no cause of action.

(b) A buys land for $125,000, represents to B that he bought it for $190,000 and sells it to B for $200,000. B may have an action for fraud. However, B must prove damages. Thus, if A can show that the land was actually worth $200,000, then B would have no damages and would not recover.

(c) Agency with a Person. If, as in the above situation, A buys land for $125,000, represents to his principal that he bought it for $190,000 and sells it to the principal for $200,000, A will have to disgorge the $75,000 profit to the principal, regardless of whether the principal was actually damaged, because A, the principal's agent, owed him a fiduciary duty: "Unless otherwise agreed, an agent who makes a profit in connection with transactions conducted by him on behalf of the principal is under a duty to give such profit to the principal" (RLA § 388).

One difficult issue that courts have had to struggle with is the question concerning who should keep funds or goods that were improperly obtained through one's agency position. Courts have held that principals have the right to seize the improperly obtained funds. For example, when bribes are obtained through one's agency position, the funds are to be given to the principal. In *Reading v. Regem* (King's Bench 1948), the plaintiff obtained bribes by using his station in the British army. When the British government discovered what had happened, it seized the money and the plaintiff sued to recover it. The court held that, because the money was obtained through the plaintiff's uniform and position as the Crown's servant, the money belonged to the Crown.

If an agent unjustly diverts business from the principal for his own profits, he becomes liable to the principal in damages. In *General Automotive Manufacturing Co. v. Singer* (Wis. 1963), the defendant solicited the plaintiff's customers for his side business in a way that diverted business from the plaintiff. After the defendant left, the plaintiff sued to recover the defendant's profits. The court ruled in favor of the plaintiff, since the defendant worked at an additional job that was the same kind as the plaintiff's business and in so doing, caused detriment to the plaintiff. There would have been nothing wrong if the agent had informed the principal of his intentions and obtained the principal's approval, but here, he did not do so.

2.4.2   "Grabbing and Leaving"

(a)   An agent's fiduciary duties apply not only during the period of the agency, but also, after its termination. An agent who leaves his employment thus may not use insider information to which he had access during the employment to his profit and to the principal's detriment.

(b)   Courts treat the insider information to which agents have access as *trade secrets* to which the principal has an exclusive right to commercially exploit. For example, in *Town & Country House & Home Service, Inc. v. Newbery* (N.Y. 1958), the defendant employees, after leaving their jobs with the plaintiff, used the plaintiff's customer lists to solicit business to a separate, competing cleaning service company that they formed. The plaintiff sued for an injunction. Holding that the defendants' use of the plaintiff's lists in forming their own company constituted unfair competition, the court granted the injunction.

3 Accounting and Finance

The principles discussed in this chapter relate to accounting and finance, both of which touch upon business organizations during various moments of their life cycles, from their creation to their operation and dissolution. Many of the principles described below prove key to later discussions involving choice of entity, the tax treatment of business owners and raising capital to finance business operations.

3.1 Principles of Accounting

Accounting refers to a system by which quantitative information about a business entity's finances is ascertained. It involves the preparation of a business's financial reports, which determine its debts and credits, under the standards described below.

3.1.1 Three Basic Accounting Formats

Accounting may be performed through the use of balance sheets, income statements or cash flow summaries, which together provide the foundation for most business organizations' accounting procedures.

(a) Balance sheets

Balance sheets are current statements or "snapshots," of an entity's financial state and data at a given moment. Conventionally, they are organized over three headings:

(i) *Assets:* cash, property and anything else of material value that the company owns;

(ii) *Liabilities:* debts and obligations that burden the company's equity; and

(iii) *Owners' equity:* the amount by which a company's total assets exceed its total liabilities.

(iv) Balance sheets typically do not include and cannot calculate a company's good will, reputation and intellectual property (trademarks, patents, etc.).

(b) Income statements

Income statements, also known as profit and loss statements, offer an overview of an entity's financial state over a period of time. In this way, they are unlike balance sheets, which offer a financial snapshot of an organization during a specific moment of time. Summarizing revenues (gains or increases in equity) and expenses (losses or decreases in equity) over time, income statements are generally structured as total revenue followed by a cascade of expenses.

(c) Cash flow summaries

Cash flow summaries track the movement of cash through a business and summarize how it uses cash. They illuminate changes in an entity's use of cash over a period of time. The data used in a cash flow summary comes from balance sheets and income statements.

3.1.2 Debits, Credits and Double-Entry Bookkeeping

In the world of accounting, a credit refers to anything that increases a firm's liability and a debit refers to anything that decreases that liability. Each item in bookkeeping should have a double entry, one that is recorded as a credit and another as a debit. For instance, a $100 purchase of goods is the equivalent of a $100 cash credit and a $100 inventory debit. At the end of a period, the credits and equivalent debits are closed out and net balances are transferred to financial statements. Assets are then computed by subtracting liabilities from equity.

3.1.3 Boundary Problems

Boundary problems arise when it is unclear whether certain items should be recorded in balance sheets, in income statements or whether they should even be recorded at all.

Boundary problems typically arise with respect to three kinds of entries: (i) intangible assets, including intellectual property, good will and reputation; (ii) contingent liabilities, such as lawsuits, warranties for defective items and guarantees (promises to pay another's debt in event of default); and (iii) extraordinary circumstances, including natural disasters and exceptional legal judgments. These entries and circumstances often pose challenges to accountants trying to provide accurate information on the financial health of business organizations,

3.1.4 Accounting Standards

The Generally Accepted Accounting Principles (GAAP), which are articulated by the Financial Accounting Standard Board (FASP), define approved practices for accountants in preparing accounting statements. The Generally Accepted Auditing Standards (GAAS) are a set of rules prescribing procedures that independent auditors must follow in order to certify that financial statements comply with the GAAP. Together, the GAAP and the GAAS provide accounting and auditing standards that assure that potential investors and creditors are able to work with accurate information that will assist them in making rational financial decisions as they relate to the risks and financial stability of certain business organizations.

3.2 Principles of Finance

Finance is a relatively new area of study that focuses on the allocation of scarce resources over time. It explores the costs and benefits of financial decisions that decision makers are usually forced to make with some sense of uncertainty as they try to balance the future risks and rewards of their actions. The study of finance involves a myriad of theories and principles, a few of which we will explore below.

3.2.1 The Theory of the Firm

A firm is an organization whose activities are under the discretion and authority of an entrepreneur. Corporate managers of the firm play the role of decreasing costs and increasing efficiency through moving some activities inside or outside of the firm through downsizing, mergers and acquisitions. The theory of the firm attempts to explain, based on market prices, why some of these activities are managed within the firm, while others are outsourced.

The theory of the firm recognizes the discretion of the manager as the element that distinguishes the firm from ordinary market activity. The entrepreneur is forced to find equilibrium between granting managers sufficient power to exercise discretion in order to increase profits and checking the decision making power of managers, which when left unchecked, may pursue self-interested gain over the overall profit of the company.

3.2.2 The Time Value of Money

(a) Overview

A key concept that corporate managers must come to understand is the time value of money, which allows managers to compare the current value of money with the value of the same amount in the future. Since due to inflation, any sum of money today is worth more than it would be worth in the future, managers must continually compute the time value of money when making financial decisions.

The example of settlement offers is telling. Suppose a client has the choice of receiving a $1,000,000 settlement offer today or a $1,100,000 judgment after two years of litigation. Assuming a 5% interest rate and no external factors, taking the $1,000,000 settlement today would be more advantageous than waiting, since todays' settlement offer, if immediately invested with a 5% rate of return, would equal $1,050,000 after one year and $1,102,500 after two. This, coupled with avoiding the costs and uncertainty of further litigation, make it a clear winner.

Within the context of the time value of money, an important distinction must be made between simple and compound interest. Simple interest is calculated based only on the principal; compound interest, in contrast, is calculated based on the aggregate sum of a principal and any accrued interest. Compound interest causes an investment to grow dynamically. To determine roughly how long it will take to double an investment, one may implement the "Rule of 72" by dividing 72 by the interest rate as a percentage (not as a decimal figure). For example, if a client is receiving 5% interest on an investment, he would divide 72 by 5, which equals 14.4. Thus, at a 5% compound interest rate, an investment would take roughly fourteen years to double. With a 3% interest rate, the investment would require twenty-four years to double.

(b)   Present Value of a Single Future Payment

Practitioners should also be aware of the present value of a single future payment. Suppose a client is offered the option of receiving $1,000,000 for a legal judgment within one year or receiving $960,000 today. Which is the financially preferable option, assuming a 5% interest rate? Since $1,000,000 in one year would be worth $952,380.95 today ($1,000,000/1.05), taking the $960,000 today is the financially advantageous position.

(c)   Internal Rates of Return

Finally, internal rates of return should be taken into account whenever calculating the time value of money. Suppose a client wishes to deposit $30,000 in a bank to withdraw in ten years for retirement. He can choose between: (i) a 10% compounded interest rate per year for ten years; or (ii) one single payment of $80,000 at the end of the ten years. Which option is financially preferable? To calculate the sum that the first option will give him, the $30,000 should be multiplied by $(1.1)^{10}$, the equivalent of 2.59, which represents the compounded interest rate. Since $30,000 multiplied by 2.59 yields $77,812, the second option, which will pay a $80,000 lump sum, is the preferable option.

(d)   Valuing Streams of Future Payments

Valuing a stream of future payments is similarly important to wise business decision making. Suppose a client has the option of receiving (i) $50,000 annual payments for ten years; or (ii) one lump sum of $400,000 today. Assuming an interest rate of 5%, to determine the value of ten $50,000 annual payments in today's currency, the following figures should be added together:

(i) $47,619 for the first year ($50,000 for the first year would today be worth $47,619 or $50,000/1.05%);

(ii) $43,351 for the second year ($50,000 for the second year would today be worth $43,351 or $50,000/$(1.05)^2$ or 50k/1.1025);

(iii) $43,193 for the third year ($50,000/(1.05)^3 or 50k/1.1576 or $43,193);

(iv)   …

(v)   50k/(1.05)^{10} for the tenth year.

(vi)   Added together, these figures equal $386,087 today. Thus, accepting $400,000 today would put the client in the financially advantageous position.

(e)   Conclusion

The key lesson is that, as a general rule, a sum of money tomorrow is worth less than the same sum today. Of course, in the rare and atypical situation where deflation occurs, this general rule will not hold true. Yet for ordinary economic cycles marked normal inflation rates, obtaining a lump sum today is financially advantageous over receiving the same amount in the future.

3.2.3   Other Concepts in Corporate Finance

(a)   Under the *efficient market hypothesis*, prices in financial markets reflect all available information at any time, since financial markets are "informationally efficient." The prices of traded assets are always therefore fairly based on the aggregate understanding of investors.

(b)   Whereas "return" refers to the total economic benefit of an investment over time, "risk" measures the expected variation of an investment's return. Risk can be reduced without sacrificing return via diversification. However, not all risk is diversifiable. Systemic risks, such as the possibility that a government will change a key law, remain outside of the control of the investor.

(c)   The *capital asset pricing model* helps to estimate such non-diversifiable risk. The model is based on a number called "beta." If a stock's beta is equal to 1, that stock has an average market risk; if it is greater than 1, the risk of the stock is higher than that of the market; and if the beta is less than 1, the risk is less than that of the market.

3.2.4   The Application of Double Taxation

(a)   Double taxation applies to business organizations whose profits as well as the earnings of the organizations' owners are subject to taxation. Double taxation and the costs that it implies, must be taken into account by decision makers when undertaking certain transactions.

(b)   Suppose an investor in the year 2000 purchased land for $1 million and then formed a corporation to which he contributed the land in return for all of the corporation's common stock. Because the investor merely altered the form of the ownership of the land, no federal tax liability applied to the transaction.

(c)   If, in the year 2010, however, the corporation were to sell the land for $1.6 million, taxation would apply to the $.6 million difference between the $1.6 million sale price and the $1 million substituted basis (starting point) of the investor's contribution.

(d)   Taking this one step further, suppose that the total assets of the corporation, after taxation of the $1.6 million sale, equaled $1.25. If the investor were to sell all of his stock for $1.25 million, taxation would apply to the $.25 million gain between the sale price of the stock and the substituted basis of $1 million (the value of the land originally contributed). Thus, in addition to the amount taken from the profits gained from the sale of the land, another amount would be taken from the sale of the stocks. This is what is meant by "double taxation," a phenomenon which has given rise to a series of complex operations that we will examine below that aim to minimize the burdens borne by corporate shareholders and directors.

Part II: The Sole proprietorship and Partnerships

4 Sole Proprietorships

4.1 Characteristics

4.1.1 The sole proprietorship is the most basic of the business organizations that will be explored. So basic is the sole proprietorship that some argue that it is not a business organization in the legal sense of the term, since a business organization involves the direction and ownership of at least two partners.

4.1.2 However, the name "sole proprietorship" should not mislead the reader. Certainly, the sole proprietorship is a business fully owned by one person, the sole proprietor, who holds all of the business's liabilities and assets. However, although the owner operates the business in his personal capacity, many other third parties may be involved. A sole proprietorship may involve hundreds of employees and other participants under the direction of the sole proprietor.

4.1.3 Regardless of whether it can be formally defined as a business organization, the sole proprietorship is included in this volume because it shares many of the attributes of other business organizations. The study of the sole proprietorship will therefore help build a useful foundation for the study of more complex business entities further on.

4.2 Credit, Financing and Unlimited Liability

4.2.1 The Use of Credit and Leveraging

One of the first questions that the sole proprietor will come across will be financing his business enterprise. He will be more limited than those involved in other business organizations, such as corporations, which may issue stock to finance projects.

The sole proprietor will therefore look to use credit to his advantage by *leveraging*, that is, putting up a certain degree of an investment in equity and the balance in credit. As the return on the investment increases, the return on equity will increase exponentially.

Consider the following example:

(a)   An investor puts up $25,000 in equity into an enterprise. With a 14% return, he would earn $3,500 off of the original investment.

(b)   An investor puts up $25,000 in equity in an enterprise and borrows another $75,000 in loans that he also invests. If the investment returns 14%, he will earn $14,000 on his original investment.

(c)   If the loan had a 10% interest rate, he would be required to pay $7,500 in interest. With this expense, his net gain would be $6,500, nearly twice as much as it would have been had he relied solely on equity.

(d)   Thus, even with the added expense of interest, the investor would come out ahead through leveraging, earning $6,500 off of his original equity contribution of $25,000, a 26 % gain, rather than a mere 14% gain of $3,500.

4.2.2 Taxes and Creditors

(a)   When using credit, a hierarchy of debts arises with respect to the debtor's repayment obligations. He is first required to pay taxes off of the profits of his enterprise. Second, he must pay off secured debts. Finally, he is required to pay off general debts, which are split between creditors based on the percentage of each creditor's debt interest. In recovering their loans, general creditors may go after any of a debtor's assets, except for those that are owed to secured creditors, who receive priority in the repayment hierarchy.

(b)   In an uncertain market environment, a sole proprietor who puts up a portion of the equity in an investment may never recuperate it. In an enterprise in which the profits are only enough to cover tax obligations and the repayment of secured and general debts, the sole proprietor may find that all of his work led to no gain on his original equity investment.

4.2.3   Liability

(a)   In the event that the profits were insufficient for paying off the business's debts, the sole proprietor will be held personally liable. Unlike a corporation or an LLC, the sole proprietorship does not exist as an entity distinct from its owner. It does not therefore contract its own debts and obligations and offers no corporate shell or "veil" to protect the proprietor. Any of the debts of the sole proprietorship thus become personal obligations of the sole proprietor that he must repay. His personal liability for all of the business's debts is not limited; creditors may therefore seize his personal assets, such as his home and his car, in order to recuperate their investments.

(b)   These risks, which are inherent to sole proprietorships, can be significantly reduced by forming a corporation or registering a one-member LLC, which will be explored in the chapters that follow.

4.3   Employees, Relationships and Duties

4.3.1   Although sole proprietors tend to own as well as manage their businesses, they may hire an employee to oversee the business's management. In such a case, the business would continue to operate as a sole proprietorship, since it is directly owned by one person, even though several individuals would be involved in its operation.

4.3.2   Bringing in employees and managers opens the door to many new issues, such as vicarious liability. Even when an owner (sole proprietor) is not at fault, he may be held vicariously liable for his employees' negligence when they act within the scope of their employment. One of the factors that the sole proprietor must therefore consider when hiring managers and other employees is the increased risk of liability that may arise.

4.3.3   There are several ways for an employer to reduce liability from the negligence of an employee. He can, for example, obtain insurance or limit his employee's decision making authority. One of the disadvantages of this latter option, however, is the risk of stifling a manager's ability to make profit-making decisions. In addition, limiting the manager's decision making authority may not protect the owner if a third party has reason to believe that the employee had authority to make the decision in question.

4.3.4   Another issue that may arise when bringing managers and other employees on board is loyalty. When the interests of employers and employees diverge, loyalty can be the first to be sacrificed. If an employee seeks to purchase the business, for example, he may downplay the value of the business in order to get a lower price from the owner.

4.3.5   Owners of sole proprietorships must therefore undertake a careful calculus when deciding whether to hire managerial employees and how to compensate them. To keep profits high, for example, owners may consider giving incentives, such as a share of the profits or bonuses based on the profits generated, rather than a flat salary. They must carefully draft contracts to state the limitations on the employee's decision making authority and must be careful not to make any representations to third parties that the employee's authority exceeds such limitations. They should also weigh such factors as the duration of the relationship and the risk of loss inherent in any employer-employee relationship.

5 Partnerships

5.1 Characteristics

5.1.1 Partnerships are associations of two or more individuals or "partners," who share in the management, control, profits and liability of a business. Partnerships are governed by the Uniform Partnership Act of 1914 (UPA), which has been adopted by all states except for Louisiana. The UPA treats each partner as an agent of the partnership, which may be a source of liability issues. This is especially true within the context of general partnerships, which are formed whenever two or more individuals begin a joint business operation, regardless of their intent or the lack thereof, to form a partnership. Thus, two business partners may *inadvertently* enter into a relationship where the law recognizes each as fully liable for the other's debts, torts and negligence.

5.1.2 In general partnerships, each partner is personally liable for the debts and torts of not only every other partner, but also, of *every employee under his control*. For example, if an employee acting within the scope of his employment orders an enormous quantity of perishable foods that later spoil, the partners would be bound by the employee's decision, regardless of its financial consequences.

5.1.3 Partnerships serve as a "bridge" between the law of agency and the law of corporations. The partnership is generally treated not as an independent entity, but rather, as an invisible aggregate of its individual partners. This is the approach used for determining the partnership's citizenship, taxation and dissolution. For example, unlike corporations, partnerships are not considered to be legal persons who are directly taxed under the IRC. Rather, each partner is directly taxed individually. In some respects, however, the applicable law treats the partnership as an entity,[6] rather than as an aggregate of partners.

5.1.4 Partnerships, unlike corporations, may not be sued or held liable,[7] although their partners may be. In a sense, corporations limit the liability of their directors by providing a "shield" that takes on the impact of legal judgments, protecting their directors from direct, personal liability. Only the corporation's assets (*e.g.*, computers, office buildings) may be seized and used to satisfy a judgment. In contrast, a partnership has no assets of its own and therefore, a partner may lose personal property in order to satisfy a legal judgment against the partnership. This is true even if the partner was acting within the scope of his employment when he made a business decision that caused the partnership the economic loss.

5.2 Partnership Variations

5.2.1 General Partnerships

(a) The general partnership is the traditional business organization at common law. It is created by a voluntary agreement between two or more partners to carry on as co-owners of a business for profit. Thus, at common law, the general partnership could be formed without following any corporate formalities.

(b) The partners, whose contributions may not all be equal, divide profits and losses among themselves. All partners owe broad fiduciary duties to one another and, absent an agreement to the contrary, participate in the management of the business.

---

[6] *See, e.g.*, RUPA (1997) § 207, dealing with partnerships as entities.

[7] *N.B.*: some state laws have changed this general rule and allow partnerships to be sued. The general rule may be varied according to the various modalities of partnerships, discussed below.

(c) The partners are jointly and severally liable for all debts incurred. Thus, if the assets of the general partnership do not cover a legal judgment handed down against a negligent partner, both the negligent partner as well as the non-negligent partners would be personally liable for the debt.

(d) The unlimited liability generated among the partners is one of the serious limitations of the general partnership. Much of the development of alternate business associations, such as LLPs and LLCs, has been in response to this and other limitations of the general partnership.

(e) No tax is payable at the partnership level in a general partnership. Rather, pass-through taxation applies.

5.2.2 Limited Partnerships

(a) Limited partnerships are associations with at least one general partner and at least one limited partner. While limited partners are usually passive investors without any management authority, general partners hold *control of the partnership*. All of the partners enjoy pass-through taxation, rather than double taxation, where both the business organization and the owners are taxed.

(b) General partners are personally liable for the debts and obligations of the firm. Limited partners, in contrast, have liability limited to their investment in the partnership, as long as they remain below a certain threshold of control and participation in managerial decision making. By exercising control beyond this threshold, however, a limited partner may be treated by the law as a general partner. He may thus become jointly, severally and personally liable for the partnership's debts and obligations.

(c) The technical words and language of the partnership agreement are not dispositive in determining whether a partner is to be classified as limited or general. Rather, the *actual role* that a partner plays determines whether he is a general partner for liability purposes. Thus, if a partner takes a managerial role in a partnership, it does not matter that the partnership agreement refers to him as a "limited partner." In *Holzman v. De Escamilla* (Cal. Ct. App. 1948), for example, the court held that the defendants in a firm that went bankrupt were jointly and severally liable to the plaintiff, even though they were limited partners, because of the managerial responsibility that they assumed in the firm.

(d) This rule looks to economic realities rather than titles and language in determining general partnership and is similar to the rule mentioned earlier in the discussion on agency law: it does not matter that a contract states that an individual was an independent contractor or an employee when determining whether an employer is to be liable for the individual's torts; rather, what matters is the degree to which the employer exercised control over the individual. If sufficient control was exercised, the employer will be held liable even if the employee was referred to as an "independent contractor."

5.2.3 Limited Liability Partnerships

(a) Limited liability partnerships (LLPs) are a type of general partnership in which the liability of general partners is limited. LLPs were created so that general partners who were not involved in wrongful acts would not be held liable for such acts. LLPs are created by state statutes, but not every state has recognized them. In those states that have recognized them, LLPs may be designated with varying terms, such as "professional corporations" (PCs).

(b) Although LLPs, unlike corporations, have no formal corporate veil, the LLP form shields partners from the joint and several liability inherent in general partnerships. The LLP form protects partners from both the partnership's obligations as well as from the wrongful acts of *other partners* when: (i) a certificate declaring that the firm is an LLP is filed with the state; (ii) the designation "LLP" (or another designation in states where LLPs have a different name) is appended to the name of the partnership; and (iii) the statutory requirements for the LLP are followed. When these requirements are met, each partner's liability will be limited to that which he invested into the partnership. Creditors may recover their debts from only the partnership's assets, not from partners' personal assets. A non-negligent partner in an LLP can thus lose at most that which he invested into the partnership. The partners may be statutorily required to purchase insurance in order to cover potential liabilities that arise over and above these investments.

(c)   A partner always remains *personally* liable—with his personal assets at stake—for his own negligence, wrongful acts and misconduct, as well as for the negligence, wrongful acts and misconduct of those under his supervision and control. While his liability for the wrongs of others is limited to that which he invested into the partnership, he is personally liable when he is personally at fault.

5.2.4   Limited Liability Limited Partnerships

(a)   Limited liability limited partnerships (LLLPs) are a type of limited partnership that protects general partners through offering them limited liability. Like the limited partnership, the LLLP must have at least one general and at least one limited partnership. However, whereas only the limited partners in a traditional limited partnership are protected from personal joint and several liability for the debts and obligations of the partnership, in the LLLP, both the limited as well as the general partners are protected from such liability.

(b)   The LLLP is thus like the LLP in that *all* of its partners have limited liability. However, unlike the LLP, whose formation does not require limited partners, the LLLP must have at least one limited partner as well as at least one general partner.

(c)   This form of partnership is seldom used today, since both limited partners as well as actively managing general partners could all gain personal protection against liability by incorporating the business organization or by forming a limited liability company.

5.2.5   Mining Partnerships

(a)   Mining partnerships are associations of partners for engaging in a mining business. Like general partners, mining partners share in profits, losses and debts. They have only narrow powers to bind the partnership. Mining partnerships allow for the free transfer of interests and there is no dissolution at death or in bankruptcy. The duration of the venture is defined by its scope.

5.3   The Partners

5.3.1   Partners Compared with Employees

When considering whether a business relationship constitutes a partnership, a court will consider several factors, including the following:

(a)   Whether there was *intent* to enter into a partnership, as evidenced by language in an agreement;

(b)   Whether the parties *share* in the profits, liabilities, start-up costs and losses of the business; and

(c)   Whether there is *co-ownership* and *control* of the assets of the business.

In *Fenwick v. Unemployment Compensation Commission* (N.J. 1945), the defendant Unemployment Compensation Commission ("UCC") sought to determine whether Mrs. Chesire had been an employee or partner of the plaintiff beauty salon. Although she received 20% of the profits, Chesire had been paid a salary of fifteen dollars per week and had no liability. These factors would normally indicate that she was an employee. The court thus held that she was an employee, since the plaintiff maintained control and responsibility over the salon and took ownership of all of the assets when it was dissolved. The 20% profit provision was merely a compensation scheme.

5.3.2   Partners Compared with Lenders

(a)   A lender is not considered a partner and is thus not liable to the creditors of partnerships. For example, in *Martin v. Peyton* (N.Y. 1927), the plaintiff creditor claimed that the defendant lenders were partners in a firm that owed the plaintiff creditor money. Because the defendant investors exercised close oversight of the money, the creditor argued that the investors were in fact more than lenders—they were partners. The court held that it was natural and to be expected that the defendants would closely monitor their investments, given the firm's precarious financial situation and that such oversight did not make them partners. The intent between the parties required to create a partnership was lacking. Furthermore, the defendants did not have the requisite control to be partners. The court granted judgment to the defendants.

(b)   Calling the parties "partners" in an agreement helps establish the presumption that the parties are in fact partners, but it is not dispositive. Rather, several factors will be collectively considered when determining whether a party is a lender, partner or has some other legal relationship. In *Southex Exhibitions, Inc. v. Rhode Island Builders Association, Inc.* (1st Cir. 2002), the plaintiff Southex Exhibitions alleged that the defendant was in breach of an agreement that it claimed to be a partnership agreement. Southex's predecessor originally stated there was no partnership and that Southex was merely the defendant's producer. However, since the agreement called Southex a partner and Southex shared in the defendant's profits, Southex claimed that a partnership agreement was in fact in place. The court held that no partnership existed, based on several factors, including. (i) the lack of intent to enter into a partnership; (ii) Southex's failure to file state or federal partnership receipts; and (iii) the fact that no name was ever given to the alleged partnership.

5.3.3   Partnership by Estoppel

(a)   If one party makes any representations of partnership to another party that the other party relies on to its detriment, the former is estopped from disclaiming partnership. It is the party that made representations of partnership, not the company or individual that was joined in the alleged partnership, that is estopped from denying the partnership.

(b)   In *Young v. Jones* (D.S.C. 1992), the plaintiff investor, relying on a falsified auditing document issued by "Price Waterhouse–Bahamas" ("P.W.–Bahamas"), lost $550,000 that he deposited in a bank. Upon recognizing that the documents were false, the plaintiff sued Price Waterhouse–U.S. ("P.W.–U.S."), arguing that P.W.–U.S. was P.W.–Bahamas' partner by agreement, or, in the alternative, by estoppel. The court first looked to the estoppel argument and held that partnership by estoppel could not apply, since P.W.–U.S. never made any representations to the plaintiff. The court then looked to partnership by agreement and similarly concluded that there was no partnership, since P.W.–U.S. and P.W.–Bahamas were organized separately with nothing indicating that P.W.–U.S. should be responsible for P.W.–Bahamas's liability.

5.3.4   Partnership Property

(a)   If a partner conveys his entire partnership interest to a third party, the partner retains no personal specific interest, even if the partner gains knowledge about some interest only after conveying his partnership interest. Once a partner decides to convey his interest in a partnership, he may not be able to reverse course.

(b)   In *Putnam v. Shoaf* (Tenn. Ct. App. 1981), the plaintiff sold her partnership interest to the defendants, only to later realize that her old bookkeeper had been embezzling funds. After the company sued to recover against the bookkeeper and banks that accepted forged checks, several banks paid judgments into court. The plaintiff's estate brought suit, alleging that it was entitled to recover one half of these judgments. The court held that, because the plaintiff already transferred all of her interest by quitclaim deed, she was not entitled to recover these judgments.

5.4   Binding the Partnership

5.4.1   When the partnership agreement does not state otherwise, partners may bind the partnership by majority vote. When one partner acts against the other partners' will, courts, when determining whether the partnership should be bound by the partner's acts, will question whether he was acting within the scope of the business.

5.4.2   In *National Biscuit Co. v. Stroud* (N.C. 1959), the defendant partner told the plaintiff food distributor that he would not be responsible for any more bread deliveries from the plaintiff. The defendant's partner Freeman nonetheless requested more bread, which was delivered, but the partnership did not render the payment due. When the distributor sued to recover the value of the bread, the defendant argued that since he made it clear that he would no longer be responsible for more bread deliveries, he was not liable. The court held that the defendant's partner, by accepting the deliveries, had obligated the partnership with respect to paying the plaintiff. When one partner makes a decision that is within the scope of the business, he binds the business, unless a majority vetoes his decision. Here, the defendant did not have a majority interest to veto the act—each had a one half interest. To rule in favor of the defendant partner would be to cause detriment to an innocent third party and allow the partnership a windfall. Therefore, the partnership was bound and judgment was given to the plaintiff.

5.4.3   Many state statutes allow one partner to bind the partnership only when a majority of partners vote with him. Thus, when a partnership is comprised of only two partners, one partner cannot bind the partnership over the second partner's objections. For example, in *Summers v. Dooley* (Idaho 1971), the plaintiff, against the will of his partner, hired a new employee, paid him out of pocket and later sued to recover $11,000 from the partnership funds. The court gave judgment to the defendant, who continually objected to the new employee. The court reasoned that, since there was no majority to support the plaintiff's actions, the plaintiff could not bind the partnership.

5.4.4   The different rulings between *National Biscuit Co.* and *Summers* may at first seem arbitrary. In both cases, one partner attempted to bind a partnership comprised of two partners. In the first case, the court held that the partnership was bound; in the second, the opposite conclusion was reached. Perhaps the discrepancy is due to the fact that in *Summers*, when the court ruled against the partner who hired the employee, no one was harmed besides the partner who lacked authority to bind the partnership. Compare this with *National Biscuit Co.*, where, if the court ruled against the partner who tried to bind the partnership with respect to the bread deliveries, the bread deliverer would have been unjustly harmed. The main point to take from these cases is that in cases involving only two partners, the court could potentially rule either way.

5.4.5   If a partner acts negligently within the scope of the business and causes damage to a third party, the partnership is liable. In *Moren ex rel. Moren v. JAX Restaurant* (Minn. Ct. App. 2004), the partner Nicole Moren brought her plaintiff minor son to her workplace, a restaurant where he was injured while she was making a pizza. The son, by his father, sued the partnership. The defendant restaurant brought in Nicole Moren as a third party for indemnity and contribution. Although Nicole was the sole cause of the plaintiff's injury, the court held that she could not be held liable, since she was acting within the ordinary scope of business. Thus, the partnership, not Nicole individually, was liable.

5.5   Fiduciary Obligations

The duty owed between partners is a fiduciary duty of loyalty and fair dealing. For joint-venturers, this means disclosing any information that can be read as relevant to the joint venture.

In *Meinhard v. Salmon* (N.Y. 1928), the plaintiff and defendant were partners in a joint venture. With a few months running on the lease, the owner of the land approached the defendant to offer a new lease. The defendant, without informing his partner, accepted it in the name of another firm over which he held full control. In this way, he benefitted his own firm and detrimented the joint venture. When the plaintiff found out, he sued to enforce the lease as property of the joint venture. The court held that the defendant violated his fiduciary duty when secretly appropriating the lease to himself. The dissent, however, disagreed, arguing that this case was not about a general partnership. Rather, a limited partnership lasts only as long as the lease. Under these circumstances, the defendant violated no fiduciary duty.

5.5.1   Past Partners

(a)   Partners owe a fiduciary duty only to their present, not past, partners. In *Bane v. Ferguson* (7th Cir. 1989), the plaintiff, a partner at the defendant law firm, retired and received a pension. Disaster resulted when the defendant law firm merged with another firm. Since there was no successor, the plaintiff's pension was terminated. The plaintiff sued for violation of the fiduciary duty that the defendant law firm allegedly owed him, since he was a former partner. The court held that the firm owed a fiduciary duty only to its current, not past partners and even if there was a fiduciary duty, the firm would not have violated it with respect to the defendant because the firm did not act with malice, bad faith or self-dealing. Rather, the firm partners acted in good faith with what they thought at the time would be best for the firm as a whole. Under the business judgment rule, they were not liable.

(b)   A partner owes a general duty of honesty to his fellow partners, especially when he plans to leave the partnership. The partner must disclose and not hide this information whenever it is requested.

(c)   In *Meehan v. Shaughnessy* (Mass. 1989), the plaintiffs intended to leave the defendant law firm. However, when asked, they denied their intent to leave three times. It was much later that they finally admitted their intention to leave. When asked which clients they intended to take, they did not immediately give a list. Instead, without informing the other partners, they wrote letters to all of their clients to ask them to follow them to the new firm. A couple of weeks later, the partners presented the list to the rest of the partnership. The court concluded that the plaintiffs violated their fiduciary duty through their use of the client lists. They should have been transparent with the firm and allowed the firm to send out its own letter to the clients, giving them the chance to make judgment for themselves in a more balanced way.

(d)   Expulsion of a partner from a partnership must be done in good faith. Otherwise, a violation of the partnership agreement occurs. In *Lawlis v. Kightlinger & Gray* (Ind. Ct. App. 1990), the plaintiff sued the defendant for expelling him from the firm because of his drinking problem. The court held that the firm acted in good faith and had not violated the partnership agreement because the defendants (i) gave the plaintiff two chances to reform himself; (ii) provided him with months of pay with the opportunity of finding other work; (iii) allowed him to participate in meetings and committees while he was still with the firm; and (iv) withheld nothing to which he was legally entitled from him.

5.5.2 Full Disclosure

(a) The fiduciary duty to disclose all relevant information in a timely manner does not extend to a firm's executive committee's disclosure of all details of their consultations to all partners, particularly when such details are not of value to the partnership.

(b) In *Day v. Sidley & Austin* (D.D.C. 1975), for example, the plaintiff was a partner at the defendant law firm, where he agreed to the executive committee's decision to merge with another law firm, although he did not attend any of the meetings where partners discussed the details of the merger. After the merger, however, the plaintiff found the workplace unbearable and resigned. He later sued the other partners for breach of fiduciary duty, alleging that he was defrauded as a result of the misrepresentation of key information on the merger. Summary judgment for the defendant was granted: there is no rule requiring partners to disclose information of the executive committee of this nature; nondisclosure does not amount to a breach of a fiduciary duty.

5.6 Partnership Dissolution

5.6.1 Introduction

(a) According to the UPA, dissolution is defined as "the change in the relation of the partners caused by any partner's ceasing to be associated in the carrying on as distinguished from the winding up of the business."[8] Winding up, on the other hand, refers to the liquidation of the business, where all of the assets are sold off.

(b) Termination of the partnership is one kind of dissolution. This change of relations of the partners that occurs in the termination of the partnership ends the partnership entirely. After dissolution of the partnership, there is a winding up, during which the partnership's fiduciary duties continue to apply.

(c) The right to dissolve a partnership exists whenever there are fundamental disagreements and a lack of cooperation among the partners. In *Owen v. Cohen* (Cal. 1941), severe differences arose when two partners entered a bowling business. The defendant tried dominating the enterprise, humiliated the plaintiff in front of clients and employees and took funds with neither the plaintiff's knowledge nor consent. When the plaintiff sued to dissolve the partnership, the court granted the dissolution because of the partners' fundamental differences and lack of cooperation.

(d) However, a party is unable to obtain a court-sanctioned partnership dissolution when he has breached the partnership agreement. For example, in *Collins v. Lewis* (Tex. Civ. App. 1955), the defendant persuaded the plaintiff to become a 50% partner in an enterprise that failed because of delays and rising costs. When the plaintiff sued to dissolve the partnership, he was not permitted to do so because he did not fully comply with the partnership agreement when he withheld funds and caused the enterprise to lose money. Judgment was granted for the defendant.

5.6.2 Two Kinds of Partnerships

(a) Partnerships can last for a term or can be set up to be ended anytime by any partner at will. When a partnership for a term is established, the term may be implied when it is contemplated

---

[8] UPA § 29.

that a debt will be repaid out of profits and there is an inference that the term is the period required to achieve repayment. Partnerships at will, on the other hand, can be ended at anytime by any partner. The default rule under the UPA is that any party may cancel the partnership when no definite term or particular undertaking is specified.

(b)   A partnership can be cancelled even before a profit-generating term has passed. In *Page v. Page* (Cal. 1961), for example, two partners each invested $43,000 of capital into a company. Later, when a naval base opened up nearby, the partnership turned up its first profit and the partner who was financing the operation sued to dissolve the partnership, arguing that it was an at-will partnership. The defendant argued that the plaintiff wanted in bad faith to take advantage of the new opportunity with the naval base and that the partnership should continue until the profit-generating term had passed. The court granted judgment to the plaintiff, since the defendant had not introduced any evidence of bad faith on the part of the plaintiff and since there was no evidence that the partners intended to enter into a partnership for a term.

5.6.3   The Consequences of Dissolution

(a)   Upon dissolution of a partnership, partners may purchase a company's assets at a judicially-ordered partnership sale. In *Prentiss v. Sheffel* (Ariz. Ct. App. 1973), majority partners excluded the plaintiff minority partner from the business because they were unable to get along with him. Given their good faith, the court upheld their right to acquire his 15% company interest at a dissolution sale.

(b)   Partners whose partnership was wrongfully dissolved may seek damages and carry on as though there never was a dissolution. In *Pav-Saver Corp. v. Vasso Corp.* (Ill. App. Ct. 1986), for example, the plaintiff entered into a permanent partnership with the defendant to manufacture and sell concrete machines. The agreement of both partners was required to dissolve the partnership. The plaintiff partner nonetheless unilaterally sued for a court-ordered dissolution of the company and for the return of the patents and trademarks to the plaintiff. The court concluded that the plaintiff wrongfully terminated the partnership and the defendant could carry on as though it were never dissolved. Furthermore, the intellectual property was to remain with the defendant partner (even though the agreement called for it to be returned to the plaintiff) because it was necessary to carry out the business. The liquidated damages clause for breach of contract, which was reasonable and did not operate as a penalty, was held to be valid and thus applicable.

(c)   As a general rule, partners contribute capital to and share in the profits and losses of their partnership. However, when only one partner finances the partnership, the second partner is not liable for the debts and losses of the partnership. In *Kovacik v. Reed* (Cal. 1957), for example, the plaintiff, after a joint venture failed to turn a profit, sought to split the losses with the defendant. Since both partners did not contribute to finance the operation, the defendant was not required to share in the losses.

5.6.4   Buyout Agreements

(a)   Partnership agreements may include buyout agreements that allow one partner to purchase the interests of another in the event of the latter's death or in other circumstances. Thus, a partnership is not automatically dissolved and the assets are not automatically liquidated upon the death of a partner. Consider *G&S Investments v. Belman* (Ariz. Ct. App. 1984), where the plaintiff filed to dissolve a partnership with the defendant, whose cocaine use led to bad business decisions. When the defendant died, however, the plaintiff filed an alternative complaint to acquire the defendant's interest and carry on with the partnership. The defendant's estate, which preferred dissolution and winding up, since it would have brought in more money than buying him out, argued that the plaintiff could not continue the partnership because a complaint demanding dissolution had already been filed and the partnership was thus dissolved. The court disagreed, holding that the mere filing to dissolve a partnership does not equate dissolution—there must be a legal proceeding concluding with a legal judgment. Furthermore, here, the agreement, which allows the plaintiff to buy out the defendant in the event of the defendant's death, applies. The court interpreted the agreement, which uses the term "capital account," to mean that the amount to be paid to the defendant's estate should be the value on the books, not the fair market amount.

5.6.5 Law Partnership Dissolutions

(a) Several nuances are worth highlighting in the case of law partnership dissolutions. During the dissolution of a law partnership, fees from continued legal work are to be divided according to each partner's interest in the firm, not according to the principle of *quantum meruit* (an equitable doctrine splitting proceeds according to the work put in by each partner in a given case). In *Jewel v. Boxer* (Cal. Ct. App. 1984), a law firm dissolved into two new firms and the plaintiff sued for an accounting of the attorney fees acquired during the dissolution. The court held that *quantum meruit* is not the proper doctrine to use in dividing assets; rather, the partners should continue to receive fees as they did in the former firm, regardless of which attorneys actually worked on particular cases.

(b) In discrepancies between the partnership agreement and the UPA, the partnership agreement trumps.[9] In *Meehan v. Shaughnessy* (Mass. 1989), for example, two departing partners sued to recover monies they claimed were owed to them by their law firm. The court held for the plaintiffs, reasoning that when the partnership agreement accords such rights, they ought to be enforced regardless of the UPA's terms.

---

[9] This general rule applies provided that the partnership agreement does not contravene public policy.

Part III: The Corporation

6 Introduction to the Corporation

6.1 Characteristics

6.1.1 Overview

(a) The corporation is perhaps the most economically significant of the business associations. Having origins that could be traced back to the Roman law, the corporation was by the fourth century the organization of choice for political clubs, guilds and churches. The true progenitor of the modern corporation, however, may only date back to the thirteenth and fourteenth centuries, when a coherent theory of corporation law had been developed.[10]

(b) Today, the corporation has developed into a legal institution recognized by the law as distinct from any of its owners or members. It may enter into contracts, possess property, initiate lawsuits and incur its own debts and tax obligations. The debts and assets of the corporation are held by the corporation itself, not by its shareholders. Thus, a shareholder's personal creditors may be able to obtain his corporate shares, but they may not seize the assets of the corporation itself.

(c) The corporation establishes a limited liability regime that shields the personal assets of its owners when poor business decisions cause economic losses. These losses, as well as the obligations incurred by the corporation's employees, are debts owned *by the corporation itself*, not by the corporation's owners, directors or officers. Accordingly, the creditors of an indebted corporation may seize the corporation's assets, but they may not access the personal assets of the corporation's owners, directors or officers. The corporation's shareholders risk losing only that which they invested into the corporation; their personal property and assets remain intact.

(d) Generally, there is no temporal limit for the existence of a corporation. Unless the corporate documents specify otherwise, the corporation continues indefinitely, outlasting the natural lives of any of its members. The corporation is, however, limited to those business activities established in its charter, but the scope of these activities may be broadly defined to include any lawful business enterprise.

6.1.2 Formation

(a) Corporations are formed by a relatively straightforward formal process. First, the founders must file the corporation's Articles of Incorporation with a state official who issues a certificate. State corporation codes usually require four officers (usually a president, vice president, secretary and treasurer) to then be declared. If a company does not properly follow these steps, it may default to a partnership, which carries unlimited joint and several liability to the business owners.

(b) Yet even if these formalities are not observed, courts may come to recognize a corporation-in-fact (*de facto* corporation) or a corporation by estoppel. A business organization becomes a *de facto* corporation when it behaves like a corporation and the organizers: (i) tried in good faith to incorporate; and (ii) the corporation had a legal right to incorporate. The organization becomes a corporation by estoppel when a person dealing with the firm: (i) reasonably believed it was a corporation; and (ii) it would cause a windfall if the firm was not recognized as such.

---

[10] Harold Berman, *Law and Revolution: The Formation of the Western Legal Tradition* (Harvard University Press: 1983), p. 215–221.

(c) As we will see later, another issue that courts are required to deal with is the piercing of the corporate veil—that is, disregarding the corporate form in order to achieve the personal liability of the underlying parties. Relating to this is the issue of parties' denial of a corporate form in order to renege on contractual obligations. On this question, the courts have held that when a party has notice and is aware that it is contracting with a corporation, it is estopped from defaulting on contractual obligations by denying the existence of the corporation.

(d) Consider, for example, *Southern-Gulf Marine Co. No. 9, Inc. v. Camcraft, Inc.* (La. Ct. App. 1982), where the plaintiff contracted the defendant to build a ship. In the original agreement, the parties decided that the plaintiff company would be incorporated in Texas. The plaintiff was later incorporated in the Cayman Islands. In an action by the plaintiff to enforce the contract, the defendant argued against the plaintiff's corporate existence at the time of entering into the contract, since the plaintiff did not incorporate as agreed to in the contract. The court held that the defendant knew of the plaintiff's legal status at the time that the defendant entered into the contract and the defendant agreed to the plaintiff's being incorporated in the Cayman Islands. The court held in favor of the plaintiff: the defendant may not use the plaintiff's legal status to renege on its contractual obligations. Because the defendant was unable to show that the plaintiff's being incorporated in the Cayman Islands, as opposed to in Texas, affected the defendant's substantial rights, the defendant was required to perform its contractually-stipulated duties.

6.1.3 Control

(a) Control within corporations tends to vary according to their size. Whereas in small corporations, the owners tend to be the group that controls the corporation, in most large corporations, control tends to be hierarchical: shareholders elect the board of directors, who in turn elect or appoint the corporation's officers (chief executive officer, chief financial officer, etc.), who must act with board approval before undertaking major decisions.

(b) The ownership and control of most large corporations is thus separated; while the shareholders own the corporation, the board and professional managers hold control. Shareholders do, however, exercise a certain degree of control, since they vote for the board members and may vote in favor of or against certain "fundamental matters," as defined in the corporate governing documents.

(c) However, not all shareholders may exercise the right to vote. Normally, corporations issue both common and preferred stock. Common stock grants the stockholder voting rights, whereas preferred stock gives the stockholder priority over the distribution of dividends or of company assets upon dissolution, thus protecting investor returns without necessarily conferring voting rights.

(d) In large corporations, the board is generally self-perpetuating. Since there are often thousands of stockholders, especially in the larger American multinational corporations, it can be difficult for them to come together in an organized fashion to vote for fundamental changes of policy or leadership. A problem may thus arise when managers pursue their own interests and objectives to the detriment of the shareholders. Thus, to align the interests, shareholders may award managers performance-based pay in the form of stock options or profit-based bonuses. This helps align their interests with those of the owners by giving them the incentive to make profit-generating decisions.

(e) Yet even this solution has shortcomings. For example, if a manager knows that he will be involved in a corporation for a limited time and part of his compensation package involves stocks, he may make decisions that will benefit the short term value of his shares without considering the long term well-being of the corporation and of its stockholders. As an example, consider the 2001 Enron fiasco, where managers sought to inflate the short term value of their stock options through a scheme that ultimately brought great financial loss to one of America's largest companies.

6.1.4 Double Taxation

As already mentioned, corporations are legal entities recognized by the law as persons that generate their own tax obligations. This leads to double taxation, since the earnings of the owners of the corporation, in addition to the corporation's own profits, are subjected to taxation.

6.2 The Internal Affairs Rule

6.2.1   Under the approach adopted by the majority of states, a corporation, regardless of where it operates or where its shareholders or assets are located, is bound by the laws of the state of its incorporation. Under the principle known as the "internal affairs rule," the laws of the state of incorporation will govern the corporation's internal affairs (how the corporation is run, the recourse for resolving conflicts between owners and managers and similar questions).

6.2.2   As a consequence of the internal affairs rule and because a vast number of corporations choose to incorporate in Delaware because of its favorable corporate tax regime, Delaware corporate law is applied by courts throughout the country whenever a Delaware corporation is the subject of a lawsuit. However, in some states, such as California and New York, corporations registered in other states are required to conform to local state laws under certain circumstances.

6.2.3   Although some states' rules are more permissive than others', all states have laws that permit "foreign" corporations—corporations registered in another state—to operate in their territory. Usually, this requires identifying an agent for service of process in the event that the corporation is sued and paying a fee and local state taxes. For example, in order for a corporation registered in Delaware to operate in Missouri, the corporation would be required to select an agent for service of process and pay Missouri taxes and fees.

6.3 The Scope of Corporate Purpose

The directors of a corporation have broad discretion in running the corporation, but this discretion must be exercised primarily to maximize the pecuniary gains of the corporation's shareholders. In exceptional circumstances, the directors may undertake charitable contributions and other acts not directly related to maximizing shareholder gains. These acts are, however, governed by a series of principles under the "rule of reason," which limits the extent to which directors may make charitable contributions from the corporation's profits.

6.3.1   *Intra Vires* Transactions

(a)   An *intra vires* transaction is one that is within the power and authority of a corporation or individual. Corporations may, for example, be authorized to make charitable contributions, even when their corporate charters do not expressly allow this right. When the donation promotes the objectives of the corporation, it is said to be *intra vires*. In *A.P. Smith Mfg. Co. v. Barlow* (N.J. 1953), the plaintiff, a manufacturer of valves, fire hydrants and other special equipment, made a gift to Princeton University in the amount of $1,500. The defendant stockholders argued that the gift was not authorized within the corporate charter. The court held that the charitable contribution by the plaintiff was *intra vires:* the power to make a donation is implicit whenever the corporation can show that the donation is within the corporation's interests. In the present case, the corporation argued that supporting private liberal education indirectly and ultimately benefits corporate culture.

(b)   While corporate directors may exercise discretion in deciding whether to distribute dividends to shareholders or to reinvest profits back into the corporation, they may not distribute profits to charitable ends without giving consideration to their duty to profit the corporation's shareholders. In *Dodge v. Ford Motor Co.* (Mich. 1919), the plaintiff minority shareholders argued that the defendant Ford Motor Company's withholding of dividends from shareholders was arbitrary and that its use of profits as capital to expand the company was inconsistent with the best interests of the corporation. It was concluded by the court that, in the absence of bad faith, courts of equity would not interfere with the right of the directors of a corporation to distribute dividends, determine their amounts or reinvest profits back into the corporation. Thus, the court did not enjoin the plaintiff from expanding its business. However, the court also held that the defendant could not distribute its corporate profits for the benefit of the public at large by reducing the prices of its cars, since the primary purpose of a corporation is to provide profits for its shareholders. Thus, a decree ordering the defendant Ford Motor Company to pay $19.3 million in dividends was upheld.

(c)   However, when business judgment is exercised, courts will not interfere with corporate directors' decisions to balance the profitability of an enterprise with other considerations, such as the well-being of the surrounding neighborhood of the enterprise. In *Shlensky v. Wrigley* (Ill. App. Ct. 1968), the plaintiff brought a derivative action against the defendant director for refusing to install lights that would allow the Chicago Cubs to play night games. The plaintiff argued that the defendant's failure to install lights negatively impacted the profitability of the corporation and was wrongly motivated by a concern for the good of the neighborhood, rather than of the shareholders' profits. The court concluded that, even if the plaintiff could show that the installation of lights and the introduction of night games would generate increased revenue, there was no showing of fraud, illegality or conflict of interest in the defendant's decision and therefore, the defendant was protected under the business judgment rule. The case's dismissal was affirmed.

6.3.2   *Ultra Vires* Transactions

(a)   An *ultra vires* transaction (occasionally referred to as *extra vires*), in contrast with an *intra vires* transaction, goes beyond the authority granted by a corporate charter or by law. Any fraudulent or illegal decision or one that involves a conflict of interest is categorized as *ultra vires*. The failure to operate within the scope of both state law and the corporation's articles of incorporation will give rise to an unenforceable *ultra vires* act or contract.

(b)   A corporation that is sued to comply with a contractual obligation may raise the defense that the contract imposes an *ultra vires* obligation that is accordingly unenforceable. However, many state statutes preclude corporations from raising this defense, since doing so would benefit and protect a corporation that wrongly undertook an *ultra vires* obligation. The defense may be further rendered inapplicable by corporate charters that state purposes so general (*e.g.*, "to engage in any lawful business") that any legal transaction could be reasonably characterized as *intra vires*.

6.4   Corporate Modalities

6.4.1   Closely Held and Public Corporations

(a)   Corporations may be public or closely held. In a closely held corporation (also termed "close corporation"), there is no ready market for shares. Rather, the corporation is usually owned by a small group of individuals who also manage the corporation and serve on its board. With relatively modest economic scopes, closely held corporations are not subject to the same formalities as public corporations.

(b)   Public corporations, in contrast, issue shares of stock that are owned by the public at large and that are actively traded on stock exchanges, such as the NYSE and the NASDAQ. The existence of public markets enables public corporations to raise capital and permits shareholders to quickly liquidate their ownership through transferring their shares to interested buyers. In addition to issuing stock, public corporations may raise capital by issuing bonds or debentures, which, like stocks, may be held or traded. The issuance of these securities, as well as the markets in which they are traded, are extensively regulated by federal law.

(c)   The ability to quickly liquidate ownership and raise capital through public stock markets does not exist in closely held corporations, which are not owned publicly and whose shares are generally not traded. This is in part due to the lack of demand for shares of such corporations.

6.4.2   Loan-Out Corporations

Loan-out corporations can be used by high-income individuals, such as professional athletes or entertainers, to achieve tax benefits. The loan-out corporation is formed to take in the individual's income and distribute it to the individual in the form of a salary and fringe benefits, such as health insurance or retirement savings. This offers important fiscal savings, since the funds disbursed as fringe benefits will be exempted from taxation. Only those funds distributed to the athlete or entertainer in the form of a salary from the loan-out corporation will be subject to taxation.

6.4.3   Startup Corporations and Venture Capital

(a)   One of the challenges that any startup corporation faces is collecting sufficient finances to underwrite its costs. One source of funding that entrepreneurs may look to is venture capital. Wealthy individual investors or pension funds may contribute venture capital to invest in the early stages of start-ups to help promising entrepreneurs launch corporations and other ventures. In return, the investors hope to earn substantial returns in exchange for the high risk inherent in investing in startup companies.

(b)   Venture capital managers bargain for a share of participation in control and may seek various protections, such as a veto power over the management's decisions. Having *de facto* control over the entrepreneurial group, they are not considered passive investors.

7 Obligations of Directors and Officers

7.1 Liability and the Business Judgment Rule

The liability of a corporation, like that of any entity, is never limited in any way. Corporations have unlimited liability for all of their legal obligations and can be required to satisfy these obligations to the extent coverable by their assets.

7.1.1 General and Limited Partners

(a) Before defining and examining the business judgment rule and its application in questions of corporate liability, it is important to understand the distinction between general and limited partners of limited partnerships, particularly in cases in which corporations serve as general partners of the limited partnership.

(b) The general rule of limited partnerships is that while limited partners are liable only up to the amount that they invested, general partners may be held personally liable for the partnership. However, beginning in the 1960s, lawyers developed a variation on the limited partnership in which a corporation serves as the sole general partner. In this structure, no individual is liable for the debts of the partnership: the limited partners enjoy limited liability and the owners of the corporation are shielded by the corporate veil and corporate characteristics of limited liability.

(c) One question that arises is whether a limited partner that engages in the management of the corporate general partner of a limited partnership, as an officer or director, can be held personally liable. The answer for many courts has been "no."

(d) In *Frigidaire Sales Corporation v. Union Properties, Inc.* (Wash. 1977), for example, the plaintiff argued that the defendant limited partners should be held liable as general partners of a limited partnership, since, as shareholders, directors and officers of the limited partnership's corporate general partner, they exercised control of the corporation. The court disagreed, holding that limited partners do not incur general liability for the general partner's obligations, even if they are owners, directors or officers of that general partner. This would not be the case if the limited partners assume powers going over and above their rights as limited partners or where there is a showing of fraud or deception and formalities with respect to the corporation serving as the general partner are not observed. Here, this was not the case. The judgment in favor of the defendant was affirmed.[11]

(e) However, other courts have held that a limited partner may be held liable as a general partner if his or her acts constitute control of the limited partnership.

7.1.2 The Business Judgment Rule: Application and Rationale

(a) Although they may be held personally liable for their personal torts and other wrongful acts, corporate directors and officers are protected under the business judgment rule for business decisions that are within the scope of their employment and made in good faith and with a reasonable investigation. Business decisions that fall within the business judgment rule are thus not actionable, even if they cause economic harm to the corporation or to third parties.

(b) The business judgment rule is based on the rationale that the courts are unable and unwilling to evaluate the risk and return calculus implemented by directors and officers when making

---

[11] *N.B.*: other states may have held these limited partners liable because they **exercised control** over the corporation.

business decisions. The courts do not wish to scrutinize the management's business decisions or to impose their own judgment as to whether the directors acted reasonably, particularly when the directors are experts in their respective economic sectors. In *Kamin v. American Express Co.* (N.Y. 1976), the plaintiff shareholders brought a derivative action against the defendant, seeking damages for a wasteful dividend in kind in the form of shares of a company that the defendant purchased at a great loss. The defendant corporation judged that, if it simply distributed the value of the shares in kind, as opposed to selling the shares on the market, it would have avoided losing credibility as a result of its loss. The plaintiffs argued that the defendant should have sold the shares in order to offset its loss with an $8 million tax saving. The court held that it would not question the directors' business judgment, even if it caused financial loss to the shareholders. Since the plaintiffs failed to show a failure of good faith or of reasonable investigation, the case was dismissed.

7.1.3   Inapplication of the Business Judgment Rule

The breach of the duty of care of a director or manager constitutes an act of negligence that triggers personal liability and the inapplication of the business judgment rule. The breach of the duty of care can be caused by:

-    a lack of good faith or of reasonable investigation;
-    negligence and other tortious conduct lacking business judgment;
-    a failure to establish oversight; or
-    acts implicating a conflict of interest.

(a)   Lack of Good Faith or of Reasonable Investigation

When the plaintiff meets his burden of proving a lack of good faith or of reasonable investigation, the business judgment rule will not apply and corporate officers or directors may be held personally liable. The case *Smith v. Van Gorkom* (Del. 1985) offers an example of a grossly negligent failure to undertake an investigation such that the business judgment rule failed to apply. In *Smith*, the plaintiff shareholders brought a class action lawsuit against the board members for accepting an offer to purchase the corporation without making a reasonable investigation as to whether the $55 per share price offered was an accurate representation of the value of the company. The court found that the officers relied on the CEO's representations without availing themselves of all available information. The business judgment rule did not protect the defendants because they failed to make a business judgment and instead acted with gross negligence. The fact that the shareholders later approved the sale did not change this result.

(b)   Negligence and Other Tortious Conduct

The business judgment rule only protects a director or officer when he exercises business judgment (*i.e.*, when a business decision is made). It does not apply to acts of negligence and other tortious conduct where no judgment or decision is made, even if such conduct is neither fraudulent nor illegal. Personal liability may arise, for example, when an officer or director negligently fails to direct or to supervise. For example, in *Francis v. United Jersey Bank* (N.J. 1981), Lillian Pritchard, the defendant shareholder and director of Pritchard & Baird Intermediaries Corporation, was held personally liable for failing to supervise and direct her two sons who misappropriated $12 million from the corporation's trust accounts, proximately causing the clients' loss. The business judgment rule was held to be inapplicable.

(c)   Failure to Establish Oversight

The directors of a corporation have an affirmative duty to establish oversight procedures and assure that corporate information and reporting systems are adequate. The absence of such oversight constitutes a breach of the duty of care that triggers the personal liability and inapplication of the business judgment rule. If, in contrast, reasonable oversight is present and management tries with good faith to ensure that reporting is adequate, the business judgment rule will apply, even if the oversight fails to identify improper behavior.

Consider, for example, *In re Caremark International Inc. Derivative Litigation* (Del. Ch. 1996), where Caremark, a managed health care provider, entered into contracts with doctors and hospitals for consultations and research, without first clarifying the unsettled law on prohibited referral fee payments. When the government investigated Caremark and indicted two officers, several shareholders filed derivative actions against the board of directors for failure to monitor. The court found that Caremark directors had been making adequate efforts to centralize control and monitor employees and were therefore not liable, even though they failed to detect the officers' misconduct.

(d)   Conflicts of Interest

When the business judgment rule applies, the plaintiff has a significant hurdle to overcome before he is able to win a case against a defendant director or manager. However, when there is an unratified conflict of interest, the business judgment rule would not apply and the burden would shift to the defendant director or manager to prove that the decision was *reasonable* and *fair*. See, for example, *Bayer v. Beran* (N.Y. Sup. Ct. 1944), where the president of the defendant Celanese Corporation of America engaged in a $1 million per year advertising campaign in which he contracted his wife as a singer. In a suit charging negligence and waste, the business judgment rule did not apply, since self-dealing was involved. The president had the burden of proving that his decision was in the best interests of the corporation, a burden he met by showing, for example, that the singer was not paid excessively. The case was therefore dismissed.

Consider also *Lewis v. S.L. & E., Inc.* (2d Cir. 1980), where the plaintiff shareholder claimed that the defendant corporation was responsible for waste when the defendant failed to raise the rent prices on a lease it controlled. The trial court dismissed for the plaintiff's failure to show that the fair market value was not met. On appeal, the court held that because there was a personal interest for the defendant, the burden should have shifted to the defendant to prove that the rent paid was *reasonable* and of *fair market value*. The trial court was reversed, with the plaintiff entitled to an upward adjustment of his interest in the corporation.

It is important to note that this rule applies *only when the conflict of interest is not ratified by a majority of shareholders*. As we will examine below (*see infra*. "Ratification"), even if a conflict of interest exists, the business judgment rule applies when the decision in question is ratified by a majority of independent shareholders or directors.

7.2   Fiduciary Duties Generally

(a)   In general, directors owe a fiduciary duty of care to the company to which they are appointed and to its shareholders. Once elected, directors hold a fiduciary obligation to act on behalf of all of the shareholders, not just the shareholder who nominated him or her. If they vote to benefit one shareholder over the others, they have breached their fiduciary duty to the company.

(b)   A corporate director is thus required to exercise his own independent judgment and vote according to what he believes to be in the best interests of the company to which he is appointed, even if this is at odds with how the shareholder that appointed him directs him to vote. Directors are thus similar to legislators in that once they are elected, they have significant latitude to act as they perceive to be best for the company.

(c)   At the same time, however, if a shareholder owns a significant enough percentage of the company to directly elect a director, the shareholder likely can also have the director replaced by recall or through a new election.

(d)   If a director enters into an agreement with the shareholder whereby the director agrees to vote in accordance with the director's instructions, but the director fails to do so, the shareholder could try to sue the director for breach of contract. However, the chances of a court upholding such a contract are low since it contravenes the legal principle that directors must act in the best interest of the company and its shareholders.

7.3   Duty of Loyalty

7.3.1   Corporate Opportunity

Under the corporate opportunity doctrine, a corporation's directors, officers and employees owe the corporation a fiduciary duty that prohibits them from taking personal advantage of opportunities in which the corporation has a reasonable proprietary interest. An employee may not, for example, use his corporate position or information obtained from his official capacity to seize opportunities that by right belong to the corporation, unless he first makes a disclosure of the opportunities to the corporation. The law further prohibits directors and officers from taking corporate proprietary information with them when joining competitor firms. Moving between competitors is otherwise permitted, unless restricted by contract.

Various states have different rules for determining when an opportunity is considered to be a "corporate opportunity." In Delaware, the following questions are asked:

(a)   Was the corporation financially able to take advantage of the opportunity?

(b)   Was the corporation in the same line of business as that in which the opportunity arose?

(c)   Did the corporation have an interest or expectancy in the opportunity?

(d)   Would embracing the opportunity create a conflict of interest between the corporation and the personal gain of the director, officer or employee?

If he can answer these questions in the negative, a director, officer or employee who uses an opportunity for personal gain does not create an improper conflict of interest. In *Broz v. Cellular Information Systems, Inc.* (Del. 1996), for example, a corporate officer was accused of usurping a corporate opportunity by purchasing cellular telephone service for his personal corporation rather than for the corporation whose board he was a member of. The court ruled in favor of the director, recognizing that (i) the plaintiff corporation, given its bankruptcy, was in no position to purchase the service; and (ii) the plaintiff corporation was aware of the transaction and did not oppose it.

Compare the result in *Broz* with that of *In re eBay, Inc. Shareholders Litigation* (Del.Ch. 2004), where plaintiff shareholders brought a consolidated derivative action against eBay directors who allegedly usurped corporate opportunities for their own personal benefit. The plaintiffs accused the defendants of allowing Goldman Sachs, the corporations' financial advisor, to bribe them with lucrative initial public offerings (IPOs) in order to secure future business with eBay. The court denied the defendants' motion to dismiss for failure to state a claim because there was enough evidence to show that the directors were usurping corporate opportunities that rightfully belonged to eBay. Investing in securities was held to be in a line of business of eBay because eBay consistently invested a portion of its cash in securities.

7.3.2 Dominant Shareholders

(a) The *intrinsic fairness test* is a standard used to evaluate the allegation that a director or controlling shareholder engaged in an act of self-dealing. The test requires the director or dominant shareholder to show that, although he (or "it" when the dominant shareholder is a corporation) engaged in self-dealing, the questioned transaction was fair to the corporation.

(b) Under the intrinsic fairness test, the defendant is more likely to be held liable than he would if the business judgment rule were applied. The intrinsic fairness test places the burden of proving objective fairness to the corporation on the defendant, whereas the business judgment rule places a burden of proof that is usually difficult to meet on the plaintiff. The business judgment rule, unlike the intrinsic fairness test, is applied only when there is no self-dealing alleged.

(c) Consider, for example, *Sinclair Oil Corp. v. Levien* (Del. 1971), where Levien, the plaintiff minority shareholder of Sinclair Venezuela Oil Corp. ("Sinven"), a subsidiary of the defendant corporation Sinclair, brought a derivative action against the defendant Sinclair for (i) causing Sinven to pay excessive dividends; and (ii) failing to cause Sinven to pursue a breach of contract claim against the defendant. The court held that because the issue of dividends involves one of business judgment that treated all of the shareholders equally, including the plaintiff and the defendant, the business judgment rule was the proper test to apply. However, because the second issue involved self-dealing, the proper standard to have applied was the intrinsic fairness test. The case was therefore affirmed in part and reversed in part and remanded.

(d) A dominant shareholder is held to the same standard of loyalty as a corporate director. Although the dominant shareholder may vote according to his private interests, he owes the same fiduciary duties to minority shareholders that a director owes. In *Zahn v. Transamerica Corporation* (3d Cir. 1947), the plaintiff shareholder held class A shares of Axton Fisher, which came to be dominated by the defendant corporation, who later became the majority shareholder. When Axton grew in assets, the defendant liquidated class A stocks and sold assets of the corporation in order to own most of the remaining stock. When the defendant corporation dominated the board, it recalled the stock and liquidated the corporation in order to benefit the defendant corporation, which owned most of the remaining stock. The plaintiff shareholder sued, alleging that the defendant used its votes for personal gain at the expense of minority shareholders. The court agreed, holding that although a dominant shareholder has a right to control, it is held to the same standard as a director and must act according to the best interests of the shareholders as a whole. The court concluded that the defendant breached its fiduciary duty.

7.3.3 Ratification

(a) If a director breaches his fiduciary duty, he has the burden of proving fairness under the intrinsic fairness test. However, when a majority of independent, informed shareholders ratify the act, the burden shifts to the plaintiff, who must overcome the business judgment rule.

(b) However, when only a minority of shareholders ratifies the act, the business judgment rule does not apply. Instead, the defendant must prove the intrinsic fairness of his challenged act. In *Fliegler v. Lawrence* (Del. 1976), for example, the defendants argued that the burden of proof should be shifted to the plaintiff shareholders because the shareholders approved the act for which they were suing. The court first recognized that under *Gottlieb v. Hayden* (Del. 1952), the burden shifts to the plaintiff to overcome the business judgment rule when approval is granted by a majority of independent, informed shareholders. The court did not, however, apply the business judgment rule to the present case, because only 30% of the shareholders voted. The court held that the burden of proof remained on the defendant to prove intrinsic fairness.

(c)   It is important to point out that the application of the business judgment rule only shifts the burden of proof; it does not alter the fiduciary duty of the corporate officers and directors. The case *In re Wheelabrator Technologies, Inc. Shareholders Litigation* (Del. Ch. 1995) makes this clear. The plaintiffs brought a class action suit alleging that the defendant corporation Wheelabrator and its directors failed to disclose material information regarding a merger with Waste Management, Inc., thus breaching its fiduciary duty and duty of care. Wheelabrator moved for summary judgment, arguing that a majority of shareholders approved the transaction. The court held that when the majority of shareholders ratify an act, the plaintiffs bear the burden of overcoming the business judgment rule. Courts should not dismiss the case entirely when, as in this case, it is possible that the plaintiff meet its burden. Summary judgment was denied and the case was remanded for further proceedings.

7.4   Insider Information

Three distinct rules have been formulated regarding directors' and managers' duty to disclose insider information when trading:

(a)   The duty-to-disclose rule: directors holding insider information by virtue of their positions within the firm hold that information in trust for the shareholders. Directors thus have a duty to fully disclose all material information before they are allowed to trade their stocks. This applies only to information they acquire from within the firm, not from outside sources;

(b)   The no-duty rule: there is no duty to disclose insider information; liability arises only for fraud and affirmative misrepresentation; and

(c)   The special facts or circumstances rule (the "Supreme Court rule"): directors have a duty to disclose special circumstances and information that, if not disclosed, would dramatically impact stock prices.

Today, the duty-to-disclose rule is generally accepted as the standard applied in most states and more states continue to move towards this standard, which prohibits insiders from using insider information in trading stocks.

In early cases, in contrast, prior to the enactment of the Exchange Act, when securities trading was governed by the common law rather than by federal law, the rules were more lenient. *Goodwin v. Agassiz* (Mass. 1933), for instance, held that not all trading using insider knowledge was prohibited, particularly when such trading was not fraudulent. In Goodwin, the defendants purchased shares of Cliff Mining, Co. The defendants made the purchase while having some insider knowledge, specifically, the untested theory that they were about to discover minerals on the land. They did not disclose this information because they wanted their other mining corporation to acquire adjacent land. After the purchase, the stock's value significantly increased and the plaintiff former shareholder sued for breach of fiduciary duties and loss of profit arising from defendants' failure to disclose the information. The court held that the fiduciary duties of directors should not be so onerous as to require every director who seeks to buy or sell a share to disclose everything that he knows about the corporation to the person with whom he is trading; such requirements would deter skilled, experienced individuals from accepting office. Here, the defendants did not withhold the information fraudulently; they were not certain whether the minerals would be discovered. To make such an announcement prematurely could generate liability if they turned out to be wrong. Furthermore, there is no evidence of fraud and the plaintiff was no novice, but rather, an experienced trader who of his own volition decided to sell the shares.[12]

A higher standard was established by the Exchange Act and the SEC Rules. The purpose of SEC Rule 10b-5 is to level the playing field and to assure that insiders and outsiders have access to the same information and opportunities when trading securities. The statutory rules require disclosure of all material insider information before trading or refraining from trading. A fact is considered material when a reasonable person would attach importance to it when making decisions in trading securities.

In *Securities & Exchange Commission v. Texas Gulf Sulphur Co.* (2d Cir. 1968), for example, the defendant corporation instructed its employees to keep an ore strike a secret. The employees proceeded to trade the corporation's stocks with this material insider information. When rumors of the massive ore strike reached the press, the defendant initially denied the existence of the ore strike, but later confirmed it. This caused the defendant's stock value to rise over a brief period from $17 to $58 per share. The SEC sued the corporation's employees for insider trading as well as the corporation for its misleading statements to the press. The court held that it is unlawful to trade on material insider information until such information has been publicly made available to all investors. Anyone who has access to such insider information, whether or not he is a director, must under Rule 10b-5 either disclose such information to the investing public or hold off from trading for personal gain. Here, the information was considered "material" because for a reasonable person, it would have a "substantial effect on the market price of the security if ... disclosed." The defendant's employees were therefore engaged in insider trading in violation of Rule 10b-5.

The different outcomes in *Texas Gulf Sulphur Co.* and *Goodwin* can be attributed to several factors. In *Texas Gulf Sulphur Co.*, the defendant deliberately misled the public in denying the ore strike. In contrast, there was no evidence of such deceit in *Goodwin*. Furthermore, the defendant's knowledge of the strike in *Texas Gulf Sulphur Co.* case was certain, whereas in *Goodwin*, it was based merely on a theory. Finally, the knowledge in *Texas Gulf Sulphur Co.* was material.

If an insider gives nonpublic information to a tippee who then transmits this information to the public, the tippee may be held liable if he knew or had reason to know that the insider was gaining a benefit from the tippee's conveyance of the information. In *Dirks v. Securities & Exchange Commission* (U.S. 1983), Secrist, an insider of Equity Funding of America (EFA), tipped off the defendant with insider information that EFA was engaging in fraud by falsely inflating EFA's value. The defendant tippee verified this information by speaking with EFA's officers and employees and later informed the financial community, which led to massive liquidations and value losses of EFA security holdings as well as convictions of EFA officers for fraud. The SEC then indicted the defendant for violating § 10(b) of the Exchange Act by openly disclosing nonpublic information and tipping off investors. The court disagreed, holding that a tippee is not liable for spreading information he receives from an insider when the tippee does not know or has no reason to know that the insider gains a benefit from the insider information going public. Here, the insider received no benefit from the information's going public and he had already left EFA at the time. The defendant tippee therefore did not derivatively breach § 10(b) of the Exchange Act. Judgment for the plaintiff was reversed.

If an insider uses insider information for his personal gain, he is misappropriating information that properly belongs the company. Such misappropriation violates SEC Rule 10b-5. In *United States v. O'Hagan* (U.S. 1997), the defendant was an attorney for the law firm of the client Grand Metropolitan PLC (Grand Met), which retained the defendant's law firm to represent it in a tender offer (a public invitation to corporate shareholders to tender their shares to the offeror at a given premium) of the common stock of the Pillsbury Company. The defendant attorney, who was not assigned to the case, learning that Pillsbury

---

[12] Today, with the Exchange Act and the SEC Rules in place, courts would likely come to a different conclusion.

stock would be offered, purchased shares at $39 each. When the offer was announced, the stock was worth $60 per share. The defendant, after selling his shares and making over $4 million, was indicted on fifty-seven counts of fraud, money laundering and misappropriation of information. The federal government claimed that he misappropriated information entrusted to him by using it for his personal gain, thus violating Rule 10b-5. The government also claimed that Rule 14e-3(a), which prohibits an individual from buying or selling shares in a tender offer when he possesses material nonpublic information, was violated. The court agreed, affirming the traditional rule that directors, officers and others in a fiduciary relationship with a corporation who possess material, nonpublic information have a duty to either refrain from trading or to disclose their information publicly before trading. The judgment was awarded to the plaintiff.

7.5   Piercing the Corporate Veil

Whenever it becomes apparent that the corporate form creates a conflict of interest or is used to perpetrate a fraud or other illegal act, a court may "pierce the corporate veil" to impose personal liability for a corporation's obligations on the corporation's officers, directors or shareholders, whose liability would otherwise be limited. As discussed below, the operation of the corporation as an "alter ego" is a required element of piercing the corporate veil.

7.5.1   Elements Required for Piercing the Corporate Veil

The corporate form will be disregarded and the corporate veil pierced, thus giving rise to the personal liability of individual officers, directors or shareholders:

(a)   Operating a corporation as an alter ego (*i.e.*, without observing legal formalities and with no legal separation between the owners and the company);

(b)   Recognizing the corporation as a separate entity would further a fraud, injustice or inequity.

Both elements are required in order to pierce the corporate veil; merely operating a corporation as an alter ego, if there is no underlying fraud, injustice or inequity, is insufficient grounds for some courts to pierce the corporate veil.

In *Sea-Land Services, Inc. v. Pepper Source* (7th Cir. 1991), the plaintiff sold peppers to the corporate defendant, but was unable to collect payment because the defendant was dissolved and held no assets. The plaintiff, suing to pierce the corporate veil and hold the sole shareholder of the defendant liable, won summary judgment, but was reversed on appeal. The court held that although it was clear that the defendant was an alter ego, with funds being transferred to and from the corporation, the plaintiff failed to show the level of *injustice* required for the court to pierce the corporate veil. An unsatisfied default judgment on its own is not sufficient for a court to pierce a corporate veil.

In some states, operating a corporation as an alter ego in such a way that furthers some inequity, even if it is non-fraudulent, is a sufficient basis to pierce the corporate veil. In *In re Silicone Gel Breast Implants Products Liability Litigation* (N.D. Ala. 1995), for example, the plaintiffs brought a class action lawsuit against defendant Bristol Meyers for injuries suffered because of acts by the defendant's subsidiary Medical Equipment Corporation (MEC). The plaintiffs argued that Bristol, the sole shareholder of MEC, should be held liable. On Bristol's motion for summary judgment attacking the plaintiffs' failure to offer sufficient evidence for fraud, the court held that a jury could conceivably find that MEC was in fact the defendant's alter ego and that the nature of the present action in tort did not require a showing of fraud. Even if a showing of fraud, misconduct or inequity were required, the plaintiff could conceivably show that protecting the corporate veil could lead to inequity, since MEC had insufficient funds to meet claims against it. The defendant's motion for summary judgment was therefore denied.

7.5.2   Cases Where the Corporate Form was Preserved

(a)   When a corporation is being run separately from the assets of the managers and from those of other parent corporations without any intermingling of funds, the corporate veil will be preserved. See, for example, *Walkovsky v. Carlton* (N.Y. 1966), where the plaintiff was struck by a cab operated by the defendant cab company owner. The defendant was the sole shareholder of ten different cab companies, each which owned only two cabs. Since the defendant held only minimum insurance for each separate corporation, the insurance would not have covered the plaintiff's judgment. The plaintiff thus sought to pierce the corporate veil and hold the defendant personally liable. Because there was no illicit intermingling of funds and each corporation was operated separately, the court refused to pierce the corporate veil and held that the defendant should not be penalized for taking out minimum insurance in a way that complied with the law.

(b)   A parent company is liable for the negligence of its subsidiaries. However, one subsidiary cannot be held liable for the torts of other subsidiaries merely because they share a common parent company. The corporate veil of one subsidiary may not therefore be pierced in order to satisfy the liability of another subsidiary. See *Roman Catholic Archbishop of San Francisco v. Sheffield* (Cal. Ct. App. 1971), where the plaintiff sued the defendant, arguing that the defendant was liable for a Swiss Catholic group's failure to deliver a St. Bernard dog, since the Catholic Church worked as one corporate body and hierarchy. The court held that while one could argue that the Pope may be liable as a principal for the Swiss Catholic Group's negligence, the principle of *respondeat superior* could not apply to two equally situated subsidiaries.

(c)   Awarding a generous termination package, absent a showing of gross negligence, illegality or fraud, will not on its own trigger the piercing of the corporate veil. Rather, the decision will fall under the protection of the business judgment rule. In *Brehm v. Eisner* (Del. 2000), the plaintiff and other stockholders sued Disney CEO Michael Eisner when he convinced Disney President Michael Ovitz to take a no-fault termination with a $140 million termination package, despite there being evidence for a fault-based termination. The court held that it would not inquire as to whether the defendant was wasteful in awarding an exceedingly lucrative package or in agreeing to a no-fault termination when there was evidence of fault. The defendant may have been intentionally avoiding expensive litigation that a fault-based termination may have generated or he may have been using good faith business judgment in ways that exceed the scope of a court-based probe and evaluation. The dismissal was thus affirmed.

7.6   Indemnification and Insurance

7.6.1   Since corporate directors may find themselves entangled in potentially frivolous lawsuits, they would have little incentive to take their jobs if their corporations did not agree to indemnify them for their court costs and legal fees in the event of such lawsuits. Many corporations thus agree to provide such indemnification or to otherwise advance reasonable costs involved in defending such actions. In order to incentivize directors to comport themselves legally and with due care, board member agreements often indemnify directors only when they prevail in their lawsuits. Some agreements, in contrast, go as far as indemnifying directors for legal fees and costs even if they do not prevail in lawsuits and to pay judgments entered against them. For corporate officers, in contrast, the general practice is to indemnify only legal fees and only in the event that the officer prevails in a lawsuit. Legal fees may be provided directly by the corporation, though the more general practice is for fees to be advanced to directors and officers liability insurance taken out by the firm.

7.6.2   Several cases demonstrate this trend. In *Waltuch v. Conticommodity Services. Inc.* (2d Cir. 1996), the plaintiff Norman Waltuch was sued for fraud in an antitrust case after the silver market crashed. In defending himself in lawsuits, he had generated over $1 million in legal fees and achieved settlements or dismissals. After being fired as part of a settlement with his former employer, the defendant corporation Conticommodity Services, Waltuch sought indemnity from Conticommodity under the Delaware General Corporation Law and Article 9 of the corporation's articles of incorporation. The court held that the plaintiff was entitled to indemnification because he was vindicated through the cases' dismissal and settlement. Under Delaware's General Corporation Law, if an officer is vindicated on a legal claim on the merits, he is entitled to indemnification, even if the result achieved is settlement or dismissal; a showing of good faith is not required.

7.6.3   The General Corporation Law of Delaware permits corporations to enter into agreements with directors whereby the corporations advance litigation fees in lawsuits involving directors. In *Citadel Holding Corporation v. Roven* (Del. 1992), for example, a former director sued to require the defendant corporation to advance legal expenses associated with an agreement that the former director entered into with the defendant that entitled the former director to advancement of legal fees in suits against him. The defendant corporation argued that it was not required to make such payments because the agreement made an exception to suits brought under § 16(b) of the Exchange Act .[13] The court distinguished between the right to indemnification and the right to advance payment of legal fees. In this case, even if the plaintiff ultimately did not have a right to be indemnified, his legal fees should be advanced under the agreement, which required the defendant to advance reasonable costs involved in defending such actions. Judgment for the plaintiff was awarded.

---

[13] Section 16(b) is intended to allow the issuer of a security to recover a profit on the security when it was achieved by an officer or director unfairly using information obtained by virtue of his relationship to the issuer.

8   Corporate Accountability

Among the methods that can be used to achieve corporate accountability, we will explore the following: (i) the appraisal right; (ii) takeover bids; (iii) securities monitoring; and (iv) derivative litigation. In addition, proxy contests and other techniques for obtaining control of a corporation, which will be examined in the following chapter, can also be considered as methods for achieving accountability.

8.1   The Appraisal Right

8.1.1   The Appraisal Right is a statutory right protecting shareholders who may be dissatisfied with their corporation's merger. It is only available when the corporation undergoes a statutory merger or a court treats a merger cast in some other form as statutory.

8.1.2   Shareholders may seek an appraisal right that requires the corporation to pay them the fair value of their stock. Absent an agreement as to the fair value of the shares, the value may be determined by a judicial proceeding. This remedy is seldom sought by shareholders because it is very expensive and it ties up their stock for as long as necessary until the legal process is resolved.

8.2   Takeover Bids

8.2.1   In a takeover bid, an offer is made to buy stock at a premium price, often at fifty to one hundred percent over the market price. There are two kinds: (i) *hostile takeover bids*, where the board of directors and the management (not necessarily the shareholders) oppose the takeover; and (ii) *friendly takeover bids*, where the board and the management support the takeover.

8.2.2   In a hostile takeover bid, the board may seek the intervention of a friendly bidder, referred to as a "white knight," to rescue it from the "black knight" (unfriendly bidder) through offering a more appealing offer. In addition to the white knight and the black knight, a "gray knight" may enter the equation with an offer that is more favorable than the bid of the black knight, but less favorable than that of the white knight.

8.2.3   The takeover bid poses a problem of coercion. When there is a two-tier tender offer, the high price initially offered diminishes as the bidder continues to purchase more shares. Thus, shareholders feel compelled to sell their shares immediately in order to avoid inevitably less attractive offers later on. Due to its coercive nature, this form of takeover is prohibited in many states.

8.2.4   Takeover defense tactics may involve measures known as "shark repellants" that a company may take in advance as well as after a tender offer is made in order to make hostile takeover attempts more difficult to achieve. Examples of such tactics include corporate charter provisions requiring that a merger or sale of the company be approved by a supermajority of voting shareholders and "poison pills," which give shareholders the right to buy shares of the surviving corporation at a discount if the merger is not approved by the board, thus making the target company's stock less attractive to the acquirer.

8.3   Securities Monitoring: Disclosure and Fairness

8.3.1   Definition of a Security

Section 2(1) of the Securities Act of 1933 ("Securities Act") defines *securities* as belonging to one of two categories: (i) stocks, bonds, notes, etc.; or (ii) evidence of indebtedness, investment contracts or "any instrument commonly known as a security." Knowing whether the object of a transaction is a security is necessary for determining whether federal registration laws and the anti-fraud provisions of the Securities Act apply.

For example, in *Robinson v. Glynn* (4th Cir. 2003), the plaintiff sued the defendant companies, alleging fraud when the defendant sold the plaintiff a partial interest in a company. The plaintiff claimed that the partial interest was either a stock or an investment contract. The court held that the partial interest did not qualify as an investment contract, since the plaintiff was not a passive investor dependent on others' interests. Furthermore, it was not a stock, since the members did not share in profits in proportion to the number of shares they held. The case was therefore dismissed.

To qualify as *stock*, an interest must be negotiable and able to be pledged and the shareholders must share in profits. To qualify as an *investment contract*, the Howey four-factor test applies, requiring:

(a)   A common scheme or enterprise (pooled resources);

(b)   An investment of value; and

(c)   An expectation of profit; that

(d)   Is solely (or predominantly) derived from the efforts of others.

8.3.2   Securities and Exchange Commission Monitoring

(a)   Two distinct securities markets are regulated by state and federal law: (i) the primary market, which deals with securities that are issued by corporations to investors for the first time (as in the case of IPOs); and (ii) the secondary market, where formerly issued securities are exchanged or traded, among investors via stock exchanges. Companies may accumulate millions of dollars of liquid capital through the primary market by issuing securities in the primary market. These securities are then traded among investors in the secondary market through stock exchanges, such as NASDAQ.

(b)   These markets are regulated extensively by both state and federal law. On the federal level, the United States Congress has passed the Securities Act and the Securities Exchange Act of 1934 ("Exchange Act"), both of which set forth rules designed to benefit and inform investors and protect them from fraud.

(c)   The Securities Act is a registration and disclosure statute that deals mainly with the primary securities market. Signed into law by President Franklin D. Roosevelt after the Great Depression, it was aimed at increasing trust in American markets through the registration and disclosure of important financial information. Focusing on the "primary market," it enabled investors to purchase the quantity and quality of risk desired.

(d)   The Exchange Act, dealing mainly with the secondary market, forms the basis of financial market regulation. The Exchange Act is mostly an anti-fraud regulation with various disclosure and other regulatory requirements. In addition to banning fraud, it regulates tender offers and proxy contests and requires publicly traded companies to regularly disclose financial information. The Act aims to level the playing field by allowing outsiders to trade with the same information that insiders hold. It created the Securities and Exchange Commission ("SEC") to enforce federal securities law by investigating and prosecuting violations.

(e)   On the state level, several laws regulate both primary and secondary securities markets. "Blue sky laws," for example, protect prospective shareholders from fraudulent speculative schemes having "no more basis than so many feet of 'blue sky.'"[14] These state laws, which require sellers

---

[14] As cited by Justice McKenna in *Hall v. Geiger-Jones Co.*, 242 U.S. 539 (1917).

to register their offerings of securities, sometimes conflict with federal regulations. To avoid such conflicts, some states have adopted the Uniform Securities Act, a model statute dealing with securities law and securities fraud.

8.3.3   The Registration Process

(a)   Under the Securities Act of 1933, before a corporation may make an IPO of stock, it must as a general rule file a registration statement with the SEC, which must in turn declare the registration statement effective.

(b)   Some securities are entirely exempted from this requirement. Other securities, while not entirely exempted, may be exempt if made as "private placements" under § 4 of the Securities Act. A private placement is one where the offering is relatively small and is limited to a small group of sophisticated investors. In order for this exception to apply, each offeree must be furnished with or must have access to information about the corporation that he would have received had the corporation filed a registration statement.

(c)   In the case of private placements, even if an IPO is small and made to a small number of sophisticated investors, the corporation must deliver to each offeree the same information that a registration statement would have disclosed or the IPO will be held to be invalid. In *Doran v. Petroleum Management Corp.* (5th Cir. 1977), the plaintiff sued for violation of the Securities Act and the Exchange Act. On appeal, because the record did not show that the corporation delivered to each offeree the same information that a registration statement would have disclosed, the judgment for the defendant was reversed in part and the case was remanded.

(d)   Under § 11 of the Securities Act, it is unlawful to commit fraud and make untrue statements in connection with the sale of securities through a registration statement. If § 11 of the Securities Act is violated, the issuer of the security as well as anyone who signs, the directors of the corporation and those about to become directors, every expert who gives an opinion with their identified consent and any underwriter of the security, will be held liable. The plaintiff does not need to plead reliance or causation in establishing his *prima facie* case. Rather, his case consists only of showing: (i) a false statement was made; and (ii) the statement was material (referring to matters of which an average prudent investor ought reasonably to be informed before purchasing the security that was registered).

(e)   The defendants (all but the issuer, who has no defense) may offer the defense that their misconduct did not cause the plaintiff's harm or that they acted with due diligence. Under § 11 of the Securities Act, the due diligence defense is available whenever the defendant, before making any misrepresentations, affirmatively studies the statement by making a reasonable investigation and comes to believe that the statements are true. The standard is objective in that it takes into account what a prudent business manager would come to believe and subjective in that it requires that the issuer of the statement to actually believe the statement. In *Escott v. BarChris Construction Corp.* (S.D.N.Y. 1968), the defendant corporation issued debentures to finance its bowling alley construction business. The plaintiff, a purchaser of debentures, sued the defendant for furnishing materially false information on the statements. The defendants moved to dismiss by raising the defense of due diligence. The court held that the defendants did not successfully prove their defense: the directors provided auditors with incorrect information and relied on information provided by officers, rather than conducting their own due diligence through an independent investigation. Being new comers was no defense and the motion to dismiss was denied.

(f)   Section 10(b) of the Exchange Act provides the following:

It shall be unlawful for any person, directly or indirectly, by the use of any means or instrumentality of interstate commerce or of the mails or of any facility of any national securities exchange ...

(b) To use or employ, in connection with the purchase or sale of any security registered on a national securities exchange or any security not so registered ..., any manipulative or deceptive device or contrivance in contravention of such rules and regulations as the Commission may prescribe as necessary or appropriate in the public interest or for the protection of investors ...

(g)   This is meant to protect the integrity of the market by proscribing "false or misleading statements." Thus, while simply not commenting or responding to questions is permitted, false, fraudulent or misleading statements are prohibited. This is designed to protect an environment where investors may assume that market prices are not contaminated by false or misleading information and that corporations are not manipulating market prices.

(h)   Section 10(b) also proscribes insider trading. Those who profit from the knowing possession of non-public material, as well as those who knowingly aid or abet them, are liable under the Exchange Act. The Act proscribes such behavior in order to assure that all people have that same information and are on a level playing field. Triple damages are imposed on those who are convicted under the Act. Thus, for every $1,000 in profits illegally made, $3,000 in damages is imposed.

(i)   Perhaps the most important of the SEC Rules is Rule 10b-5:

It shall be unlawful for any person, directly or indirectly, by the use of any means or instrumentality of interstate commerce or of the mails or of any facility of any national securities exchange,

(a) To employ any device, scheme or artifice to defraud,

(b) To make any untrue statement of a material fact or to omit to state a material fact necessary in order to make the statements made, in the light of the circumstances under which they were made, not misleading or

(c) To engage in any act, practice or course of business which operates or would operate as a fraud or deceit upon any person,

in connection with the purchase or sale of any security.

(j)   Proving a violation of SEC Rule 10b-5 requires showing that the following elements are met:

    (i)   **Jurisdictional Means**. The purchase or sale of a security must be made through the use of "interstate commerce or the mails" (Rule 10b-5);

    (ii)   **Fraud**. This includes knowing manipulation and deceitful acts and statements.

    (iii)   **Materiality**. The misrepresentation must have been as to a material aspect of the purchase or sale. A representation is material when a reasonable shareholder would consider it important when buying or selling a security.

(iv) **Scienter**. The defendant must have knowingly and intentionally misled the plaintiff. Negligence is insufficient, but recklessness meets the standard.

(v) **Standing**. The plaintiff must have purchased or sold securities.

(vi) **Causation.** This element requires that the fraud cause the plaintiff's pecuniary loss.

(vii) **Reliance.** The plaintiff must have relied on the defendant's misleading statement when entering into the transaction.

(k) There is a rebuttable presumption that a shareholder relies on a representation whenever he buys or sell shares. See *Basic Inc. v. Levinson* (U.S. 1988), where the court provided an analysis of the material misrepresentation and reliance elements of Rule 10b-5. In *Basic Inc.*, the defendant corporation engaged in merger negotiations with Combustion Engineering, Inc., but publicly denied doing so three times. The plaintiff former shareholders then initiated a class action lawsuit, seeking certification based on the presumption of relying on the defendant's misrepresentation. The court held that determining the materiality of the representations requires a case-by-case review of the facts in order to determine whether a reasonable investor would have relied on the representations. In a case where an event is only speculative, a reasonable investor probably would not rely heavily on it. The case was remanded in order for the lower court to determine the probability of the consummation of the merger with Combustion Engineering, Inc. On the issue of reliance, however, the court affirmed the lower court in holding that there is a rebuttable presumption that plaintiffs rely on material public misrepresentations in class action lawsuits and that defendants have the burden of overcoming this presumption.

(l) Section 10(b) of the Exchange Act requires that the defendant not be engaged in "any manipulative or deceptive device or contrivance." There is, however, no private cause of action for a mere breach of duty absent fraud. In *Santa Fe Industries, Inc. v. Green* (U.S. 1977), the defendant corporation, owning 90% of Kirby Lumber's stock, decided to merge with its subsidiary Kirby in order to eliminate minority shareholders. The plaintiff shareholder sued under § 10b of the Exchange Act of 1934 and Rule 10b-5 of the SEC, based on the theory that the merger took place without notice to the minority stockholders and that it was not for a business purpose. The court held that if minority stockholders wished to pursue a cause of action for an unfair price of the stocks purchased, they ought to pursue state remedies, such as a court appraisal, since the Exchange Act does not allow such causes of action absent fraud.

(m) On the contrary, a cause of action arises under § 10(b) of the Exchange Act for knowing misrepresentation. The cause of action arises even when the corporation and its officers have no fiduciary duty to the purchaser. An investor may sue the corporation or its officers not only when the investor has purchased stocks or call options (the right to purchase stock when it reaches a certain price). In *Deutschman v. Beneficial Corp.* (3d Cir. 1988), the defendant corporation sold the plaintiff call options, which the plaintiff claimed lost value because of misrepresentations of co-defendants Casperson and Halvorson, the defendant corporation's officers. When the true value of the defendant corporation was discovered, the plaintiff's options lost value. The appeals court held that the fact that there was an intentional misrepresentation that affected the plaintiff's investment was enough to give rise to a cause of action. In addition, Congress, the SEC and the Federal Reserve System have all had a role in treating options contracts as securities. They are therefore to be protected as such. Finally, insiders need not be engaged in trading in order to harm the value of a purchaser's call options. Misrepresentations on their own can cause the options to lose value. For all of these reasons, the judgment for the defendants was reversed.

(n)   The following chart summarizes the implementation of § 10(b) of the Exchange Act through Rule 10b-5 of the SEC:

§ 10(b) (Exchange Act)	Rule 10b-5 (SEC)
"It shall be unlawful for any person, directly or indirectly, by the use of any means or instrumentality of interstate commerce or of the mails or of any facility of any national securities exchange . . .	"It shall be unlawful for any person, directly or indirectly, by the use of any means or instrumentality of interstate commerce or of the mails or of any facility of any national securities exchange,
"(b) To use or employ, in connection with the purchase or sale of any security registered on a national securities exchange or any security not so registered . . .	"(a) To employ any device, scheme or artifice to defraud, [in connection with the purchase or sale of any security.]
"any manipulative or deceptive device or contrivance in contravention of such rules and regulations as the Commission may prescribe as necessary or appropriate in the public interest or for the protection of investors . . ."	"(b) To make any untrue statement of a material fact or to omit to state a material fact necessary in order to make the statements made, in the light of the circumstances under which they were made, not misleading or "(c) To engage in any act, practice or course of business which operates or would operate as a fraud or deceit upon any person,"

8.4   Shareholder Derivative Litigation

8.4.1   Introduction

(a)   Shareholders may sue on behalf of a corporation to redress violations by corporate officials of duties owed to the corporation if the board fails to take appropriate action. The actions are called "derivative" because the shareholders derive their right to sue from the corporation itself. In a derivative action, the shareholder sues the corporation in equity in order to force the corporation to sue the corporate officials who violated their duties. The corporation is thus only a nominal defendant; the true defendants are the officers or board members committing the wrongs at hand.

(b)   Because these suits are driven by attorneys, there is a great likelihood of collusive settlements of small damages with significant fees. This is nevertheless a better option for the corporation than a full-blown trial that can cost far more than a settlement.

8.4.2   Posting Securities in Derivative Actions

(a)   If the plaintiffs are successful in a derivative action, the corporation reimburses them their costs. However, if they are unsuccessful, they may become liable for the expenses that the corporation incurred in the action. The United States Constitution does not prohibit statutes that make unsuccessful plaintiffs in derivative actions responsible for these expenses. In *Cohen v. Beneficial Industrial Loan Corp.* (U.S. 1949), when the plaintiff brought a derivative action, the defendant

Beneficial Industrial Loan Corp. called for the plaintiff to post a bond of $125,000 under a New Jersey statute requiring plaintiffs with less than a 5% or $50,000 interest in a corporation to pay reasonable attorneys' fees if they are unsuccessful in a lawsuit. The plaintiff challenged the statute as unconstitutional. The court held that stockowners owe a fiduciary responsibility to their corporations and it is neither unreasonable nor unconstitutional to demand reasonable attorneys' fees in unsuccessful litigation. The state may therefore impose standards of responsibility on stockowners who bring derivative actions by requiring the plaintiffs to post security. Cases may be dismissed when the plaintiffs fail to post the required security.

(b)   However, when plaintiffs sue corporations on their own behalf, as opposed to derivatively on behalf of the corporation, a court may not dismiss the action if they fail to post bond. In *Eisenberg v. Flying Tiger Line, Inc.* (2d Cir. 1971), the plaintiff sued the defendant corporation for surreptitiously depriving the plaintiff and other minority shareholders of voting rights. The lawsuit was dismissed when the plaintiff did not post security to the corporation. The plaintiff argued that, since he was bringing a class action lawsuit, as opposed to a derivative action, he was not obligated to post security. The court agreed: a derivative lawsuit, unlike the present suit, is one that is brought in the right of the entire corporation.

8.4.3   The Requirement of Demand on the Directors

There is a general rule that requires that stockholders, before bringing a derivative lawsuit, demand that the corporation's board of directors bring suit. When the stockholders fulfill this duty, two possibilities arise:

(a)   The board agrees with the stockholders, in which case it deals with the problem directly by bringing suit. The shareholders drop out of the picture;

(b)   The board disagrees with the stockholders and refuses to sue.

In the second case, the decision of the board not to sue will be protected by the business judgment rule. If the shareholder nonetheless decides to sue, he must overcome the burden of showing fraud, self-dealing or some other wrongful activity on the part of the board. There is a presumption that the board acted with reasonable judgment, which the plaintiff must disprove in order to recover. In *Grimes v. Donald* (Del. 1996), the plaintiff shareholder wrote to the board requesting that the board abrogate some of the defendant corporation's agreements, which the plaintiff claimed to have led to excessive compensation. The court held that after the board refused the plaintiff's demand, a rebuttable presumption of reasonable business judgment arose on the board's behalf. Even if the management made a bad or faulty decision, they can still defend themselves on the basis of the business judgment rule. They may, for example, argue that solving the problem raised by the shareholders would mean undergoing substantial expenses and causing more harm than the original problem posed. Such an argument would in fact protect their decision not to act.

The stockholders are not always required to make a demand on the board; doing so would not be necessary if the stockholder could show that it would be futile. Such would be the case if the board was engaged in fraud or self-dealing or if the board was being asked to return funds that it had embezzled from the corporation. A demand would similarly be futile whenever the majority of directors are not disinterested in the transaction or when the underlying conduct was improper under the business judgment rule. *Marx v. Akers* (N.Y. 1996).

8.4.4   The Role of Special Committees

(a) Special committees are often appointed by corporations when they must decide whether to allow a derivative action to go forward. The business judgment rule applies to the special committee whenever it is composed of disinterested, independent members. When evidence is submitted showing that members of the committee had prejudicial interests, the decision to block the derivative litigation will not stand. In *In re Oracle Corp. Derivative Litigation* (Del. Ch. 2003), for example, the plaintiffs brought a derivative action against four of Oracle's directors for assuring the public that Oracle would meet its guidelines, even though they allegedly knew that Oracle would fail. Oracle appointed a special litigation committee (SLC) composed of two Stanford professors to determine whether to go forward with the action. The SLC made a motion to terminate the action, but this was denied because of evidence showing that the SLC's independent judgment was compromised. This evidence included a $50,000 donation that one of the defendants made to Stanford University, one half of which was to be used for the research of one of the members of the SLC. The court thus recognized the possibility of the SLC's bias in dealing with the defendants.

(b) The fact that a special committee is comprised of members of the board of the defendant corporation is not on its own enough to challenge the committee's independence. In *Auerbach v. Bennett* (N.Y. 1979), the plaintiff shareholder sued General Telephone and Electronics Corporation (GTE) for its involvement in worldwide bribery. GTE appointed a committee of three disinterested board members who joined the corporation after the alleged bribery to decide whether the derivative action should be allowed. The special committee decided that it should not and argued the same and won in a hearing for summary judgment. The plaintiff appealed, arguing that the committee should be held to be legally infirm, given its members' interest in the action. The court held that the decision of the committee was proper under the business judgment rule and that there was nothing to indicate prejudice or bias on their part. To exclude all of the board members from making the decision as to whether a derivative action should go forward would be to paralyze the corporation from exercising business judgment.

(c) In a minority of states, the approach to the business judgment rule is more stringent. In these states, it is not enough for the committee members to prove only that they did not act fraudulently, illegally or with a conflict of interest. The Court also imposes its own business judgment rule on the facts to determine whether it would have arrived at the same conclusion as the committee. In *Zapata Corp. v. Maldonado* (Del. 1981), the defendant corporation created an independent committee comprised of two new directors to determine whether to allow a derivative action to go forward. When the committee concluded that it should not, the plaintiff sued the management. On the corporation's motion to dismiss, the court held that the corporation did not have power through the business judgment rule to dismiss the present action. When evaluating whether a committee properly prevented a derivative action, a court must consider (i) whether the committee acted independently, without personal interest and in good faith; and, if so, (ii) whether the corporation's conduct meets up with the court's own reasonable business judgment. The case was allowed to move forward on remand.

9   Problems of Control

9.1   The Special Context of Closely Held Corporations

Because the owners of closely held corporations do not have a ready market in which to sell their shares should they disagree with the corporation's management, case law and statutes have evolved to offer special protections in the areas of control and abuse of control of closely held corporations.

9.1.1   Overview

(a)   The common law and state statutes have recognized the right of shareholders of closely held corporations to enter into agreements to vote jointly to multiply their voting power in electing directors or steering corporate policies. Such agreements are necessary for shareholders to secure their investments where no ready market is available should they wish to exit. The courts have repeatedly held that such agreements are a valid tool that shareholders may use in exercising influence over closely held corporations. In *Ringling Bros.-Barnum & Bailey Combined Shows v. Ringling* (Del. Ch. 1947), for example, the plaintiff and Aubrey Ringling Haley (the codefendant) agreed to always vote jointly in a corporation of three shareholders and submit to arbitration in the event that they disagreed. When a disagreement arose as to whom should be voted to the board of directors, Haley breached the contract and voted on her own, arguing that the previous agreement was void. The court disagreed, holding that agreements by shareholders to vote jointly are valid. Because Haley breached the agreement, a new vote was ordered and Haley's votes were not to be counted.

(b)   The courts have also held that agreements to vote jointly are valid not only with closely held corporations, but with other corporate forms as well. In *Ramos v. Estrada* (Cal. Ct. App. 1992), the plaintiff and the defendant director entered into an agreement with other stockholders of the Broadcast Group to vote according to the majority of the Broadcast Group in making decisions. When the defendant defected from a vote, the plaintiffs voted to have her removed from the board and the defendant declared the agreement void. The court held that owners of stock may agree to vote by proxy to run a corporation in a way that the majority decides and to elect the managers of their choice. Although such agreements have generally been used within the context of closely held corporations, they may also be used by other corporate forms, such as the Broadcast Group, which was not closely held. The judgment for the plaintiff was affirmed.

(c)   The courts have restricted the validity of such agreements when they tie the hands of the board of directors once they are elected. Shareholder agreements may not therefore relate to the election of officers, the salaries of directors and other issues that directors must be free to decide on using their own independent judgment once elected. In *McQuade v. Stoneham* (N.Y. 1934), the plaintiff, then a city magistrate, entered into an agreement with the defendant majority shareholder of the New York Giants when the plaintiff purchased shares from him. The agreement preserved their roles as officers and directors and set the salaries of the officers. When disagreements arose and the plaintiff was discharged from his role as an officer, the defendant and McGaw (codefendant) abstained from voting on the board, breaching the agreement. The court held that although stockholders may enter into agreements in deciding how they will vote, they may not enter into agreements that bind how the officers will act, what their salaries will be and other issues relating to the independent judgment of the directors. The power of directors to manage a corporation, select agents for the corporation at set salaries and act in its best interests may not be limited by shareholder contracts.

(d)   The strict *McQuade* approach was modified two years later in 1936 in *Clark v. Dodge* (N.Y. 1936), where the same New York court held that agreements between shareholders that bind the directors to vote in a certain way for particular officers are valid *when the shareholders and the directors are the same group of people*. In *Clark*, where the sole shareholders were the directors of the corporation, an agreement circumscribed the role and actions of plaintiff minority shareholder (also a director) and provided that the defendant majority shareholder would succeed the plaintiff as director. When the defendant breached the agreement, the plaintiff sued for enforcement and the case was dismissed. On appeal, the court held that the agreement as to who would serve as officers was valid. Unlike in *McQuade*, here, the owners and directors are the same people and there is therefore no concern that the shareholders are interfering with the management. The agreement, which neither harms nor injures any third parties, is valid.

(e)   The *Clark v. Dodge* decision has been replicated and fleshed out by other courts. *Galler v. Galler* (Ill. 1964) held that agreements among the owners of a closely held corporation concerning corporate management will be held valid when agreed on by the owners and the management, there is no injury to minority interests, the public or creditors and there is no evidence of fraud or statutory violation. In *Galler*, the court upheld a shareholder agreement and held that the owners in a closely held corporation where the owners and the management are the same may bind the management when it can be shown that there is no fraud or disadvantage to minorities.

9.1.2   Abuse of Control in Closely Held Corporations

(a)   Although majority shareholders need room to maneuver when making decisions on the future of a closely held corporation, a balance must be struck between self-interested ownership and the fiduciary duty owed to the minority; majority shareholders must act with good faith and loyalty towards minority shareholders. In *Wilkes v. Springside Nursing Home, Inc.* (Mass. 1976), the plaintiff and three other individuals joined together to operate a nursing home. When the plaintiff was terminated from his position as director, he sued for a declaratory judgment and damages equal to lost salary. The court held that the burden of proof was on the majority in showing that it had a legitimate business purpose in terminating the plaintiff. Because there was no such evidence in the record, judgment was awarded to the plaintiff and the case was remanded to determine the extent to which remaining corporate funds should be used to satisfy the judgment.

(b)   In the *Wilkes* closely held corporation, the burden of proving a legitimate business purpose shifted to the defendant, in contrast with the business judgment rule presumption in large public corporations, where the burden is on the plaintiff to overcome the business judgment rule. In the closely held corporation, if the defendants are able to show that they acted with a legitimate business purpose, the burden would shift back to the plaintiff to prove that this was merely a pretext or that the same purpose could have been achieved in a less harmful way.

(c)   However, the status of being a minority shareholder on its own does not protect against at-will discharge when there is an agreement for at-will employment. In *Ingle v. Glamore Motor Sales, Inc.* (N.Y. 1989), the plaintiff officer sued the defendant corporation for firing him in violation of its fiduciary duties and for breach of contract. The court held that there is no implied duty of good faith and fair dealing with respect to continued employment in at-will employment contracts; such an implied duty would contravene the spirit of at-will employment, which could be terminated at any time by either party without cause. Judgment for the defendant was affirmed.

(d)   In closely held corporations, the majority shareholders must act with complete candor towards minority shareholders and disclose all of the facts surrounding a transaction. In *Sugarman v. Sugarman* (1st Cir. 1986), the plaintiff majority shareholders sued the defendant minority shareholder for excessive self-compensation and for buying out the minority's shares at an unreasonably low price, in violation of the defendant's fiduciary duty. The court held that the defendant offered to purchase the shares at an inadequate price and overcompensated himself in order to freeze out the plaintiffs of benefits, in violation of his duties towards them. The judgment for the plaintiffs was therefore affirmed.

(e)   Various cases in Massachusetts have held that shareholders in closely held corporations owe one another the same duties that partners in a partnership owe one another. This is a fiduciary duty of the highest caliber to act in good faith and loyalty towards other stockholders and to the corporation and to refrain from acting in avarice, expediency or self-interest in derogation of this duty. Thus, when minority stockholders of a closely held corporation have the power to use their power to the detriment of others, they must act in accordance with their fiduciary duty. Even when corporate documents give minority shareholders certain powers, the shareholders must exercise them in accordance with their financial and managerial duties and not to the detriment of others.

(f)   One way that a minority shareholder can abuse his fiduciary duty is to arbitrarily and detrimentally use his veto power. Consider *Smith v. Atlantic Properties, Inc.* (Mass. App. Ct. 1981), where the defendant, owning a 25% interest, was given a veto power that he used to prevent the payment of dividends, which caused the corporation to incur a penalty tax for accumulated surplus. The other three shareholders sued to remove him, determine the dividends to be paid and reimburse the corporation for the penalty taxes incurred. The court ruled in their favor, finding the defendant's conduct to be unreasonable and that he breached his duty of good faith owed to the other shareholders. Judgment for the plaintiffs was affirmed.

(g)   The fiduciary duty of minority shareholders extends to closely held corporations whenever they intend to purchase back their own stock. They are duty-bound to reveal any material information to the stockholder before making the purchase. In *Jordan v. Duff and Phelps, Inc.* (7th Cir. 1987), the plaintiff left the employment of the defendant corporation and sold stock back to the corporation before learning of a merger that caused the value of the stock to rise. The plaintiff sued for fraud and breach of fiduciary duty. The court held that the fact that there was a company willing to pay $50 million for the defendant corporation was material information that should have been disclosed before the corporation repurchased its stock. The plaintiff was required to show that upon learning of this news, he would not have sold his stock. Summary judgment for the defendant was reversed and the case was remanded for trial.

9.1.3   Control, Duration and Statutory Dissolution of Closely Held Corporations

(a)   Because closely held corporations so closely resemble partnerships, their shareholders owe one another the same fiduciary duty of utmost good faith and loyalty that partners owe one another in a partnership. This is partially to protect minority shareholders of closely held corporations who otherwise would be unable to sell their shares at market value, since there is no readily available market.

(b)   Consider, for example, *Alaska Plastics, Inc. v. Coppock* (Alaska 1980), which demonstrates the difficulty of selling shares of a closely held corporation at a fair market value. The plaintiff, a minority shareholder in a closely held corporation, sued the corporation and its three other shareholders / directors. As part of a divorce settlement, the plaintiff received one half of the defendant director's one third interest of the defendant corporation. The plaintiff's total share was thus one sixth of the total interest. After the defendant corporation failed to notify the plaintiff of a shareholder meeting, failed to pay her dividends, refused to allow her to participate in the business and offered only $15,000 to buy her shares that were valued upwards of $40,000, the plaintiff sued to compel the defendant corporation to purchase the shares at a fair market value. The court held that stockholders in closely held corporations owe one another a duty of utmost good faith and loyalty. A remedy for breach of this duty would be dissolution, but this extreme remedy did not apply in this case, since there were no compelling circumstances. The court might also apply equity and force the majority to purchase the plaintiff's stock at fair market value.[15] However, this would not be an appropriate remedy because the corporation was not extending this benefit to other shareholders (no shareholder was permitted to sell his shares). However, because there was evidence that the defendant corporation was distributing constructive dividends while depriving the plaintiff of such payments, the case was remanded to the trial court to determine whether such dividends were being disbursed and whether Alaska law was thus violated.

(c)   California allows for the involuntary dissolution of a closely held corporation when it is necessary to protect the interests of complaining shareholders. However, mere animosity among the directors on its own is not enough. See *Stuparich v. Harbor Furniture Mfg. Inc.* (Cal. Ct. App. 2000), where the plaintiffs sued for the involuntary dissolution of the defendant corporation when disputes and ill-will arose among the directors of the family-owned closely held furniture company. The court concluded that the application of dissolution should be reserved for truly compelling circumstances, which was not the case here, notwithstanding severe ill-will and a violent confrontation among certain board members. While the furniture company continued progressing economically after losses suffered over the last decade, the remedy should not be dissolution. Summary judgment for the defendant corporation was affirmed.

(d)   Minnesota provides that in determining whether to provide equitable relief, dissolution or a buyout as relief to aggrieved shareholders of closely held corporations, the reasonable expectations rule is used: the court is to consider reasonable expectations such as a shareholder's job, salary and economic security when awarding damages. In *Pedro v. Pedro* (Minn. Ct. App. 1992), for example, three brothers each owned a one third interest in the Pedro Companies. When the plaintiff Alfred Pedro discovered discrepancies in the accounting books and an independent auditor confirmed these discrepancies, the defendant brothers fired the plaintiff. The plaintiff sued for dissolution and the defendants moved to proceed as a Minnesota buyout under their agreement, which would have entitled the plaintiff to payment of 75% of the book value of his stocks. The court held that the shareholders in a closely held corporation owe one another a fiduciary duty of good faith and loyalty, which was breached in this case when the defendants conducted themselves wrongly by, for example, firing the plaintiff, who had a reasonable expectation of lifetime employment. The plaintiff was thus awarded one third of the value of company plus his attorney's fees and prejudgment interests.

9.2   Control in Non-Closely Held Corporations

9.2.1   Proxy Contests

A proxy contest or proxy fight, is a battle of a corporate faction comprised of dissatisfied shareholders mounting a challenge against a corporation's management. The faction seeks from the corporation's uncommitted shareholders the right to vote their shares in favor of the faction's directors. The law requires the corporate faction to distribute a proxy statement and to follow an elaborate process that, given its expense and rare chance of success, is rarely pursued.

(a)   The Challenge of Mounting a Successful Proxy Contest

---

[15] *N.B.*: when determining whether the purchase of shares at fair market value would be an appropriate remedy for a breach of fiduciary duties in a closely held corporation, a court will first look to the agreement and to state law. It will only use its equity powers if it concludes that justice requires some remedy not provided for in the agreement or state law.

The difficulty in mounting a successful proxy contest can be attributed to several causes. It can be partially explained by apathy among shareholders and a natural bias towards current management. Under the "Wall Street Rule," even if shareholders were to take an active role in their investment, they would likely support the incumbent management over a group of unknown insurgents, given the tendency of institutional investors to act conservatively and avoid risk by favoring directors with a track record.

The difficulty in mounting a successful proxy contest is further exacerbated by the many advantages given to incumbent directors, who may engage corporate funds, employees and branch managers in soliciting proxies. Such solicitation is not illegal when the shareholders are informed and the funding is not unreasonably excessive. In *Levin v. Metro-Goldwyn-Mayer, Inc.* (S.D.N.Y. 1967), the plaintiff stockholders sued a defendant corporation and several of its directors for using corporate funds to pay outside organizations to solicit proxies in a contest between the plaintiffs and the defendant corporation. Reiterating that corporations may use corporate funding in soliciting proxies in a proxy contest when the funding is not excessive, the court held that the defendant's hiring a firm to send information to stockholders was a legitimate way of insuring that its stockholders were fully informed. It further held that the money spent was reasonable and fully disclosed to its stockholders and gave judgment to the defendant.

Directors may also turn to the corporate treasury for reimbursement of costs expended in defending corporate policies in *bona fide* proxy contests. In *Rosenfeld v. Fairchild Engine & Airplane Corp.* (N.Y. 1955), the plaintiff brought a derivative action against directors for funds withdrawn from the corporate treasury for defending corporate policies in a proxy contest. The court affirmed the case's dismissal, holding that corporate directors may use corporate funding to defend a policy that they believed in good faith to serve the best interests of the corporation.

Although rarely directly successful, proxy contests grant shareholders a certain degree of leveraging power, since they can bring corporation directors to the negotiating table. They may thus have the indirect benefit of pressuring directors to discuss various issues with shareholders.

(b)   Private Actions for Proxy Rule Violations

Section 14(a) of the Exchange Act prohibits the solicitation of any securities registered under the Act in a way that contravenes the rules and regulations of the Commission. Federal courts may grant all necessary remedial relief for corporate actions that violate the Exchange Act and other federal regulations. This relief includes the rescission of mergers or other acts violating the law. In *J.I. Case Co. v. Borak* (U.S. 1964), the plaintiff stockholder sued the defendant corporation, alleging that when the defendant underwent a merger, its proxy statements were false and misleading, thus violating federal regulations. The plaintiff sought rescission of the merger, damages and other equitable relief. The court held that there was a valid federal cause of action, since the plaintiff alleged the violation of federal regulations through the defendant's false and misleading statements in its proxy statements. The case was therefore remanded for a trial on the merits.

When a shareholder sues a corporation for false or misleading material information on a proxy solicitation form, he does not have to prove that he relied on the information in making his vote. When the information is material, there is a presumption of reliance. In *Mills v. Electric Auto-Lite Co.* (U.S. 1970), the plaintiff brought a class action suit to rescind a merger obtained through materially false and misleading proxy solicitations. The court held that the failure to disclose a conflict of interest between the directors of the company and the merging company was materially misleading. Because of the material element, it was presumed that the stockholder relied on the defects of the proxy solicitation.

However, the omission of valuations of option grants to outside directors based on the Black-Scholes option pricing model (a five-factor valuation formula) is not considered a violation of Rule 14(a). In *Seinfeld v. Bartz* (N.D.Cal. 2002), the defendant directors failed to include the value of option grants to outside directors in proxy solicitations. The court held that such information was immaterial for the purpose of Rule 14a-9 false or misleading statements.

(c)   Shareholder Proposals

Shareholders may recommend via shareholder proposals that the directors of the corporation take certain actions or adopt certain measures. As a general rule, the management must allow shareholder proposals to be circulated among all shareholders. There are two limitations—the first relates to who may make proposals and the second relates to the content of proposals.

With respect to the first limitation, corporations may require shareholders to have held shares for a certain period of time and to hold a certain percentage of the corporation before making proposals. Under SEC Rule 14a-8(b)(1), in order to make a proposal, a shareholder must hold at least 1% of the corporation or $2,000 in market value for at least one year by the date of the submission of the proposal.

With respect to the second limitation, SEC Rule 14a-8(i) allows management to exclude proposals when they:

(i)   Do not concern a proper subject for shareholders;

(ii)   Are illegal;

(iii)   Violate proxy rules;

(iv)   Concern a personal grievance or benefit;

(v)   Are beyond what the management may implement;

(vi)   Relate to the firm's ordinary business operations[16];

(vii)   Have been submitted in the past, but have not reached the required threshold of support; and

(viii) Relate to an operation that does not account for 5% or more of the company's total assets, net earnings and gross sales at the end of its most recent fiscal year and are not significantly related to the company's business.

Some states have carved out an exception to this rule requiring that an operation account for at least 5% of the company's assets. When a proposal raises an ethically or morally compelling issue, the requirement may be waived. For example, in *Lovenheim v. Iroquois Brands, Ltd.* (D.D.C. 1985), the defendant corporation excluded a proposal relating to the defendant's procedure in force-feeding geese to produce *foie gras* on the basis of the activity's being insignificant to the company's business (less than .05% of the company's earnings and assets were related to the production). The plaintiff shareholder argued that the social and ethical concerns made the proposal significant and compelling under SEC Rule 14a. The court held that

---

[16] See, *e.g., Austin v. Consolidated Edison Company of New York, Inc.* (S.D.N.Y. 1992) (ruling in favor of the defendant corporation when it met its burden of showing that the plaintiff's proposal involved ordinary business operations).

although the concern is economically insignificant, the moral and social dimensions are important. The defendant corporation was not permitted to exclude the proposal.

Corporations may seek to exclude proposals based on more than one of these exceptions, as did the corporate defendant in *New York City Employees' Retirement System v. Dole Food Company, Inc.* (S.D.N.Y. 1992). The defendant tried to exclude the plaintiff New York City Retirement System's proposal because it was (i) beyond the ordinary business operations; (ii) not significantly related to the company's business; and (iii) beyond what the management could implement. However, the court did not find that the defendant met its burden of proof in establishing any of these exceptions.

(d)   Shareholder Inspection Rights

(i)   The proxy rules under the Exchange Act require corporate incumbents to either: (i) provide insurgents with shareholder lists upon their request; or (ii) mail the insurgents' materials to shareholders on behalf of the insurgents. Usually, the insurgents will prefer the shareholder lists, since possessing them will enable them to directly contact whichever shareholders they wish, as opposed to having to pay for contacting every single shareholder in the corporation.

(ii)   The management is required to provide a list of shareholders when it is requested, unless it is being demanded for an improper purpose. In New York, the management would be required to provide the list to any shareholder for any business-related purpose. The desire to review a shareholder list for the purpose of making direct solicitation for a tender offer would qualify as a proper purpose. In *Crane Co. v. Anaconda Co.* (N.Y. 1976), the plaintiff stockholder sought the defendant corporation's shareholder lists in order to contact its shareholders regarding a tender offer that the plaintiff intended to propose. The court, disagreeing with the defendant's argument, held that the plaintiff's tender offer was a legitimate business purpose and that the defendant's shareholders should be free to make their decisions on the offer.

(iii)   The purpose behind demanding the shareholder list must be economic, not political, in nature. In *State Ex Rel. Pillsbury v. Honeywell, Inc.* (Minn. 1971), the plaintiff stockholder, in opposition to the Vietnam War, sought a shareholder list for the purpose of convincing the defendant corporation and its shareholders to cease productions of munitions for the war. The court, ruling for the defendant, held that the plaintiff's purpose was not related to a legitimate economic interest.[17]

(iv)   Furthermore, some states require foreign corporations to produce shareholder lists to resident shareholders when the corporations have substantial ties to the state and when shareholders have no other means of obtaining such lists. In *Sadler v. NCR Corporation* (2d Cir. 1991), the defendant Maryland corporation, which had a substantial presence in New York, tried to block the plaintiff New York corporation's tender offer. When the defendant refused to deliver its shareholder lists, the plaintiff sued. The court held that New York law required the defendant Maryland corporation to give the plaintiff New York corporation access to its shareholder lists and that this law was not in disaccord with the

---

[17] *N.B.:* if the plaintiff had not stated outright in his deposition that he was interested only in communicating his political views or if he characterized his interest as being based on a *moral issue*, he may have achieved the same positive result as the plaintiff in *Lovenheim v. Iroquois Brands* (D.D.C. 1996), who was able to make a proposal that was based on a socially important—yet economically insignificant—issue.

dormant Commerce Clause, since it applied equally to both domestic and foreign corporations and did not unduly burden foreign corporations.

9.2.2 Shareholder Voting Control

(a)   Some states allow corporations to limit voting rights by issuing nonvoting stock. This allows insiders to retain control over a corporation while permitting the corporation to raise funds. Other states allow corporations to issue stock with a limited financial interest, but do not permit the limitation of voting rights. In these states, shares of stock that limit shareholders' voting rights are deemed invalid, even though shares of stock that limit the shareholders' financial interests are permitted. In *Stroh v. Blackhawk Holding Corp.* (Ill. 1971), for example, the plaintiff shareholders sued the defendant corporation, claiming that the limitations on the financial interest of the defendant's stock were invalid. The court held that under the Illinois Business Corporation Act, the defendant could implement restrictions on its stocks, so long as voting rights were not compromised. The restrictions in question were therefore valid and judgment for the defendant was granted.

(b)   Policy rationales dictate that shareholders, in order to record objections to a vote, should not be required to participate in a shareholders' meeting. Such a requirement would be overly burdensome on both large corporations that have diverse stock portfolios and on small individual investors with limited time and means. This was the rule of law pronounced in *State of Wisconsin Investment Board v. Peerless Systems Corp.* (Del. Ch. 2000), where the plaintiff sued the defendant for breaching its duties by adjourning a corporate meeting while continuing to solicit votes in its favor and not informing the plaintiff. The defendant argued that the plaintiff was barred from suing, since the plaintiff was not present at the shareholder meeting. The court recognized that a fraudulent act would be furthered if a corporation could prevent a stockholder from suing because of his absence from a shareholder meeting if the corporation improperly excluded him from the meeting in the first place. Furthermore, requiring stockholders to be present at the meeting would violate the policy of encouraging widespread distribution of ownership, since many stockholders are unable to be present at the shareholder meetings of the diverse corporations in which they own stock. The court therefore ruled for standing in the plaintiff's favor.

9.2.3 Transfers of Control

(a)   The right of first refusal grants its holder the right to enter a business transaction with a second party according to specified terms, before that second party may enter into that transaction with a third party. Because it is contractual, the right may be structured according to terms fixed by the parties. Minority and majority shareholders may for instance agree to a right of first refusal that allows a minority shareholder, when a majority shareholder offers to purchase a minority shareholder's stocks, to refuse the offer and instead purchase the majority's stock at the same price the majority offered for the minority shareholder's stock. Such a right is to be read narrowly in transfers of the control of a company. In *Frandsen v. Jensen-Sundquist Agency, Inc.* (7th Cir. 1986), the defendant corporation was permitted under the shareholder agreement to offer to purchase the plaintiff minority shareholder's stocks. If the plaintiff refused, he could exercise the right of first refusal and purchase the defendant's shares at the same price at which the defendant offered to purchase the plaintiff's shares. The plaintiff sued when the defendant did not allow him to exercise the right. Reading the word "sell" narrowly, the court held that the defendant corporation never made an offer according to the terms of the shareholder agreement. Rather, the defendant merely restructured the corporation. The plaintiff's right of first refusal was never triggered. Judgment for the defendant was affirmed.

(b)   In the absence of bad-faith and illegality, a controlling shareholder may sell his stocks at a premium, which is a price in excess of its market value. In *Zetlin v. Hanson Holdings, Inc.* (N.Y. 1979), the plaintiff minority shareholder sued the defendant corporation for selling shares at a premium, contending that the minority shareholders should be able to share in the premium paid for a controlling interest in the corporation. The court disagreed. Here, the buyer was willing to pay extra in order to acquire influence over the corporation. Because not all of the shareholders could transfer this influence, not all of them had the right to share in the premium. Those who could transfer it had a right to the extra amount that investors were willing to pay. Judgment for the defendant was affirmed.

(c)   The sale of a controlling interest, by tender offer or otherwise, can immediately transfer the right of control. See, for example, *Essex Universal Corporation v. Yates* (2d Cir. 1962), where the defendant director of Republic Pictures, Inc. contracted to sell shares of Republic to the plaintiff and to have the majority of Republic's directors replaced with directors chosen by the plaintiff, in order to permit the immediate transfer of control. The court upheld the contract as not against public policy.

10   Mergers and Acquisitions

10.1   Introduction

10.1.1   The life of a corporation is typically terminated by its sale or merger. In the event of a sale, the corporate debts are liquidated and the corporate assets are then sold. In the case of a merger, the corporation is "absorbed" into an acquiring firm, which exchanges cash, securities or a combination of both in order to obtain the assets and liabilities of the acquired corporation. The acquired firm in a merger may continue to exist as a separate subsidiary of the acquiring firm. Since the decision to merge relates to the fundamental nature of the corporation, it often requires shareholder approval, sometimes by a supermajority.

10.2   Distinction between Mergers and Acquisitions

10.2.1   An acquisition is the takeover of one company by a second company when the purchaser clearly establishes itself as the new owner. The target company may cease to exist if all of its assets are transferred to the acquiring entity and it is then liquidated and dissolved. However, it may continue to exist if the acquisition is realized as a share transfer, in which case it continues as a subsidiary of the acquiring entity.

10.2.2   In contrast, two firms in a merger agree to go forward as a single new entity rather than remain separately owned and operated. This kind of action is more precisely referred to as a "merger of equals." Both companies' shares are surrendered and the shares of a new company are issued in its place. For example, both Glaxo Wellcome and SmithKline Beecham ceased to exist when they merged, giving birth to a new company, GlaxoSmithKline.

10.2.3   A purchase deal will be called a merger when both CEOs agree that the merger is in the best interest of their companies. However, when the takeover of the target company is hostile, the same transaction will be referred to as an acquisition. Thus, the difference between a merger and acquisition can depend on how the purchase is communicated to and received by the target company's shareholders, directors and employees.

10.3   Classification of Mergers and Acquisitions

In the examples that follow, we will consider the hypothetical acquisition of "S Corp," a fictitious small corporation, by "L Corp," a fictitious large corporation. To carry out the transaction, the parties may choose between various operations, including: (i) a Type A (statutory) merger; (ii) a "short-form" Type A (statutory) merger; (iii) a Type B informal merger; (iv) a Type C informal acquisition; or (v) a triangular (subsidiary) merger.

10.3.1   Type A (Statutory) Mergers

   (a)   Overview

          (i)   The Type A (statutory) merger is achieved by following statutorily-prescribed procedures, where a typically large corporation will acquire a comparatively small corporation, with the large corporation being the survivor (the inverse is, however, also possible). In our hypothetical, S Corp's shareholders may receive cash, shares of L Corp or a combination of both cash and shares.

          (ii)   Since the merger effects a fundamental change in the investment of the shareholders of S Corp and L Corp, the merger will generally need to be approved by the shareholders, unless the acquisition is realized through a Type B merger followed by a short-form Type A merger or by a triangular merger (*see infra.*). Shareholders who are dissatisfied with the merger are entitled to an appraisal remedy, whereby the corporation is judicially ordered to pay the shareholders the fair value of their shares, which is usually the price just before the transaction takes place.

(b) Type A "Short-Form" Statutory Merger**s**

    (i) The short-form Type A statutory merger allows two corporations to merge when one of them owns a sufficiently high proportion (generally, around 90% to 95%) of the shares of the other. In states that allow this type of merger, the procedures are simpler than those required for normal Type A statutory mergers. For example, while Type A mergers generally require corporations to undergo a shareholder vote, no such vote is necessary for short-form mergers. Corporations in some states may opt for this procedure when merging with subsidiary corporations.

10.3.2 Type B (Informal or Practical) Mergers

(a) Type B mergers are carried out independently of state law procedures—hence the denomination "informal" or "practical" merger. The merger is realized when L Corp purchases sufficient shares from S Corp shareholders to acquire control of S Corp. In return, S Corp shareholders receive cash, L Corp shares or a combination of both.

(b) Because there is no formal involvement of S Corp's board, there is no vote on the merger by shareholders of either corporation. Furthermore, there is no appraisal right for S Corp shareholders. S Corp remains intact, but once L Corp acquires a controlling interest, S Corp becomes an L Corp subsidiary. At some point, S Corp may become a part of L Corp through a Type A short-form statutory merger.

10.3.3 Type C (Informal or Practical) Acquisitions

(a) Under a Type C "informal" or "practical" acquisition, also referred to as an "asset acquisition merger," L Corp acquires S Corp's assets in exchange for cash, L Corp securities or both. Thus, unlike the statutory merger, where L Corp acquires both S Corp's assets as well as its liabilities, the Type C acquisition permits L Corp to acquire S Corp's assets without becoming the successor to S Corp's known and unforeseen liabilities. S Corp, which is left holding only cash or securities acquired from L Corp, usually then liquidates, distributing the cash and securities to its shareholders and paying off its debts. In some states, S shareholders may have to vote, since most of the assets of their investment are being sold. S Corp shareholders may or may not have appraisal right. In Delaware, for example, they would not have an appraisal right if the price of their stock were increasing.

10.3.4 Triangular (Subsidiary) Mergers

(a) The triangular merger may be used when L Corp is trying to acquire S Corp and state law requires the shareholders of both corporations to vote on the proposed merger, given the resulting fundamental change in shareholders' investment. To avoid the vote, L Corp may create a wholly owned subsidiary corporation that merges with S Corp by acquiring sufficient stock from S Corp shareholders, in exchange for L Corp stock. Although both parties to the merger must still vote, the only shareholder of the subsidiary corporation will be L Corp, which votes through its board of directors, not through its individual shareholders. Through the triangular merger, L

Corp's directors will be able to avoid the vote of its shareholders and the appraisal remedy for unsatisfied shareholders.

10.4   *De Facto* Merger Doctrines

10.4.1 The *De Facto* Merger Doctrine

(a)   Overview

(i)   The *de facto* merger doctrine provides that, even when a transaction is cast not as a statutory merger, but as a transfer and acquisition of assets, a court may treat it as though it were a statutory merger. Thus, although a transaction is not legally a merger, courts entitle shareholders to all of the traditional protections granted in statutory mergers, such as the right to a shareholder vote before the merger is undertaken and to exercise the judicial right of appraisal when they disagree with the decision to merge.

(ii)   In a mere acquisition of assets, in contrast, although the right to appraisal is granted in some states (*e.g.*, Pennsylvania), other states either do not allow the appraisal remedy or restrict its use to certain limited circumstances. As mentioned earlier, in some states, such as Delaware, the appraisal remedy is not granted for acquisitions of assets when the value of the stock is increasing and the plaintiff could obtain a better remedy by simply selling his stock. However, if a court treats an acquisition of assets as a *de facto* merger, the appraisal remedy will apply, since under Delaware law, both statutory and *de facto* mergers automatically grant dissenting shareholders the right to appraisal.

(iii) One can thus see the importance of the *de facto* merger doctrine by considering the state of Delaware. Under Delaware law, although shareholders of a corporation have a right to demand the fair value of their shares when they oppose a statutory merger, they do not enjoy this right in an acquisition of assets where the value of the stocks is not rising. Thus, by classifying such acquisitions as *de facto* mergers, thereby treating them as statutory mergers, the states are requiring the mergers to submit to the same legal requirements that apply to statutory mergers.

(b)   Test

(i)   The "practical effects test" is used in determining whether an acquisition of assets is to be treated as a *de facto* merger. The test considers whether the transfer and acquisition of assets so fundamentally changes the nature of the corporation that its identity has in fact been changed. Consider, for example, *Farris v. Glen Alden Corporation* (Pa. 1958), where the defendant Pennsylvania corporation and List Corporation, a Delaware corporation, sought to combine under a reorganization agreement whereby the defendant would acquire all of List's assets. The plaintiff sued, arguing that the defendant's shareholders were not given notice according to the statutory merger requirements. The issue was whether the transfer of all of the assets of a corporation should be treated as a statutory merger or as an acquisition of assets. The court held that although this transfer did not fulfill the formal requirements of a statutory merger, it should nevertheless be treated as such, given its practical effect in fundamentally changing the identity of the corporation. The acquisition of assets was thus treated as a statutory merger and shareholders were granted all of the corresponding rights.

(ii)   Courts may also apply equity in deciding when to treat a sale of assets as a merger. Examples of when a court will invoke its equity powers include when shareholders are not given a fair share in an acquisition. Yet under the equal dignity rule, courts are reluctant to cast an operation as a merger when it was fairly and lawfully executed as an acquisition of assets, especially if doing so would cause unnecessary litigation. In *Hariton v. Arco Electronics, Inc.* (Del. 1963), for example, the plaintiff shareholder sued to enjoin a sale of assets, alleging that the sale was really a merger disguised as a sale in order to avoid the right of fair value that Delaware shareholders have under *de facto* and statutory mergers. The court held that a valid transfer of assets should be treated as such; to do otherwise would be to subject the parties to unnecessary litigation. The equal dignity rule permits any result when the means are lawful, regardless of whether shareholders would have received better treatment if the transaction been cast in some other form. Judgment for the defendant was affirmed.

10.4.2   The *De Facto* Non-Merger Doctrine

(a)   Some shareholders dissatisfied with the results of a merger have argued that a particular transaction should *not* be cast as a merger, but rather, as an acquisition of assets. Shareholders would make this argument if, for example, under the articles of incorporation, they would have been granted a higher cash-out (buy-out) value under the principle of *redemption* (a corporation's repurchase of its securities from stockholders according to the terms of its securities agreement) than they would have gotten under a merger that forces them to sell their shares at value. The doctrine whereby a court does not treat a transaction as a merger, even though it was cast as such, is known as the *de facto non-merger doctrine*.

(b)   As mentioned above, the equal dignity rule provides that, whatever the means through which a merger is effected, it is valid when it follows the respective formalities, regardless of whether a better result for shareholders would have followed from some other operation.

(c)   In *Rauch v. RCA Corporation* (2d Cir. 1988), the plaintiff shareholders sued the defendant corporation as well as General Electric, the defendant corporation's majority shareholder, when General Electric merged the defendant corporation into itself. The plaintiffs were paid $40 per share, the amount at which the stock was valued. Had the transaction been cast as a sale of assets followed by a redemption, the plaintiffs would have been paid $100 per share under the articles of incorporation. The plaintiffs challenged the merger, arguing that the court should treat the transaction not as a statutory merger, but rather, as a sale of assets followed by redemption. The court held that in Delaware, mergers are governed by one set of rules and sales of assets followed by redemptions are governed by another. In the present case, the rules and norms required of cash-out mergers were followed. The decision declared that "the various provisions of the Delaware General Corporation Law are of equal dignity and a corporation may resort to one section thereof without having to answer for the consequences that would have arisen from invocation of a different section." The fact that shareholders would have been entitled to a greater share value under redemption does not change the fact that the transaction was legal. The dismissal of the complaint was affirmed.

10.5   Freeze-Out Mergers

10.5.1   In a freeze-out merger (also termed *cash merger*), majority shareholders acquire 100% ownership of their corporation by forcing minority shareholders of the corporation to give up their securities in exchange for cash. The majority may acquire full ownership by incorporating a second company that initiates a merger with their corporation. The majority shareholders, dictating the terms of the merger, force minority shareholders to accept cash for their shares, often through employing tender offers.

10.5.2 Certain limitations restrict the right of majority shareholders to acquire full control through freeze-out mergers. A merger is only valid when it is for the benefit of all shareholders and is based on a valid corporate purpose and a fair buyout price. Controlling shareholders may not effect a merger when their sole purpose is to freeze-out minority shareholders. Such an act would be a breach of their fiduciary duty. In *Coggins v. New England Patriots Football Club, Inc.* (Mass. 1986), the plaintiff shareholder challenged the defendant's merger, arguing that it was entered into solely for the benefit of the majority shareholder and that it was therefore unfair. The court held that there had to be a valid corporate purpose to render the merger valid. Yet here, the merger was effected purely for the benefit of the defendant, not for the corporation. However, the court did not void the merger, since doing so would be a harsh remedy in light of the fact that ten years had passed since it had been realized. The case was instead remanded for determination of rescissionary damages.

10.5.3 The merger must reveal the true value of the minority shareholders' stock. There must be full disclosure of the stock's value and the minority shareholders must be offered a fair price. In *Weinberger v. UOP, Inc.* (Del. 1983), the defendant corporation offered $21 for stock without notifying shareholders that the stock was worth $24. When the plaintiff sued to enjoin the merger, the court held that a freeze-out merger was invalid because of the lack of disclosure of the true value of the stock. Because shareholders did not have all of the requisite relevant information, they did not grant effective consent to the merger. Judgment for the defendant was therefore reversed.

10.5.4 An acquiring corporation may not delay a merger for the sole purpose of avoiding an obligation to pay a contract price. See *Rabkin v. Philip A. Hunt Chemical Corporation* (Del. 1985), where plaintiffs, arguing that a merger was delayed only to avoid a contractually obligatory price, sued to void the merger. The trial court held that the plaintiff's remedy was an appraisal and reversed the earlier dismissal, remanding the case for trial.

Part IV: The Limited Liability Company

11 Limited Liability Companies

11.1 Characteristics

11.1.1 Corporations and partnerships have traditionally served as the forms of organization from which business owners could choose. Recently, state statutes have begun to recognize a new form of business organization, the limited liability company (**LLC**), a hybrid organization that combines the advantages of pass-through taxation of partnerships with the corporate characteristics of limited liability.

11.1.2 LLCs were first recognized in 1977 by a Wyoming state statute that combines provisions taken from the laws of partnerships, limited partnerships and corporations. This innovation remained dormant until 1988, when the Internal Revenue Service issued a ruling favorable to the tax treatment of LLCs. This ruling subsequently spurred the adoption of LLC statutes in every state.

11.1.3 In many ways, the LLC bridges the law governing corporations and partnerships. Like the corporation, the LLC protects investors through limited liability equal to the amount they invest. The LLC is itself recognized as an entity with legal personality that can be the subject of debts and lawsuits, thus protecting the investors behind it. At the same time, as in a partnership, it is only the investors, not the LLC, that are taxed directly, thus avoiding the double taxation characteristic of corporations generally.

11.1.4 The LLC offers a degree of flexibility in management and ownership that surpasses that of both the partnership and the corporation. The financial interest of an LLC may be easily transferred and if a member wishes to transfer his leadership position, he may do so with the approval of the other investors.

11.1.5 Today, all fifty states have established and recognize LLCs. Although the governing legal regimes reflect some variations, all of the states have established certain common regulations. Formation of the LLC, for example, requires a state filing procedure. Once the LLC is organized, the owners, who are called "members" (as opposed to "partners" or "shareholders"), enter into an "operating agreement" that governs the organization's structure and management. Although the scope of fiduciary duties between the members within an LLC is currently unclear, it is probably similar to that within a corporation. Most LLCs are closely held, since publicly-held LLCs would be double-taxed in the same way as corporations and would thus cause their members to forfeit one of the LLC's most advantageous attributes.

11.2 Similarity to the S Corporation

11.2.1 The LLC is akin to the S corporation, which is able to escape double taxation on corporate earnings while simultaneously providing corporate limited liability. However, unlike the S corporation, the LLC is not subject to limitations as to number and type of interests. Moreover, the LLC, unlike the S corporation, may make certain partnership-like allocations of tax attributes.

11.3 Formation

11.3.1 Unlike a general partnership, an LLC cannot be inadvertently formed. Rather, its formation requires certain deliberate steps. Its members must draft the company's articles of incorporation and file them in the state in which they intend to register the company. The members must also choose a name for the company and assure that the abbreviation "LLC" appears after the name.

11.3.2 The "LLC" abbreviation serves the important purpose of protecting third parties by notifying them of important attributes about the organization with which they are doing business. Failing to append the abbreviation to the name may have materially adverse effects on a third party. For example, a third party may have a rule requiring a $1 million insurance policy when dealing with an LLC, but not with a business association that limits the liability of its owners. If the third party was unaware that he was dealing with an LLC, he may not act with the necessary prudence or protections against risk.

11.3.3 A person who fails to disclose that he is working as an agent of an LLC may be held personally liable for the company's debts. This was the case in *Water, Waste & Land, Inc. D/B/A Westec v. Lanham* (Col. 1998), where the defendants, who failed to disclose that they were working as agents of an LLC, were held personally liable for the LLC's failure to make payments .

11.4   The Operating Agreement

11.4.1 The Uniform Limited Liability Company Act (ULLCA) sets out a default layout of laws for dealing with forum, alternative dispute resolution, ownership and other issues relating to LLCs. Like all default business association rules, the default LLC rules may be contracted around by the agreement of the parties. For example, in *Elf Atochem North America, Inc. v. Jaffari* (Del. 1999), the parties entered into an agreement with an arbitration clause and a California forum selection clause. When the suit was dismissed for not having been brought in California, the plaintiff argued that the agreement invalidly contradicted the ULLCA. The court affirmed that the parties freely contracted around the default rules and that the agreement validly trumped these rules. Judgment for the defendant was affirmed.

11.5   Piercing the "LLC Veil"

11.5.1 Although not all of the case law regarding the still new LLC business organization has been established, it appears that the limited liability regimen governing LLCs will closely resemble that of corporations. In *Kaycee Land and Livestock v. Flahive* (Wyo. 2002), for instance, a trial court certified the question as to whether an LLC grants its members the same "corporate veil" treatment that a corporation grants its shareholders. The court answered in the affirmative. Thus, when legal formalities are not observed and fraud is committed, individual members do not escape liability under the shield of the entity they have created. In order to benefit from limited liability, the officers must treat the LLC as a separate legal entity and respect legal formalities, which are more flexible for LLCs than for corporations.

11.6   Fiduciary Duties

11.6.1 Courts in many jurisdictions still have not fully developed the area of fiduciary duties owed by the management of an LLC. It is therefore unclear whether the majority of jurisdictions will follow the corporate or partnership approach in establishing these duties.

11.6.2 The states are, however, generally in agreement that fiduciary duties in LLCs may be established by contract when not against public policy. As an example, the members of an LLC may permit or prohibit one another from competing with the LLC. See *McConnell v. Hunt Sports Enterprises* (Ohio Ct. App. 1999), where the court held that when an operating agreement established that a member's competing with the LLC was permitted, the member did not breach his fiduciary duty to the LLC when directly competing against it, even though he was a member, since he did not interfere with the defendant's business dealings.

11.6.3 Where the relatively new laws on LLCs do *not* define specific rights and responsibilities, courts may draw parallels with corporations by borrowing from the laws governing corporations. Thus, like owners of a corporation, members of an LLC may be ordered by a court to purchase the stock of a member as an equitable remedy when they breach their fiduciary duties towards the LLC.

11.7   Dissolution

11.7.1   Under compelling circumstances, a court, under its equity powers, may order the dissolution of an LLC. Such may be required when it is impossible for the LLC to carry on in accordance with its operating agreement due to irreconcilable differences among its members. In *Haley v. Talcott* (Del. Ch. 2004), for example, the plaintiff and defendant formed an LLC for owning property for a restaurant in which they were the sole members. After a falling out, the plaintiff sued for dissolution and the defendant argued that the plaintiff's remedy was limited to the contractual exit clause. The court held that the LLC could not continue to function in accordance with its operating agreement because the sole members were deadlocked against one another and the LLC could take no actions absent a majority vote of its members, who in this case each held a fifty percent interest in the restaurant. The LLC's dissolution was therefore necessary and summary judgment was granted to the plaintiff.

11.7.2   A member of an LLC must respect statutorily prescribed rules regarding formation, dissolution and creditor notice in order to enjoy the protections provided by the law. In abiding by these rules, the member will avoid personal liability for the debts of the LLC upon dissolution. Otherwise, personal liability will lie. See, for example, *New Horizons Supply Cooperative v. Haack* (Wis. Ct. App. 1999), where the plaintiff creditor sued the defendant debtor for the balance of credit that was never paid. The defendant argued that, having charged the credit as a member of a dissolved LLC, she should not be held personally liable. The court disagreed, holding that the defendant did not observe legal formalities, such as giving creditor notice and properly dissolving the LLC. Therefore, she was held personally liable and judgment was granted to the plaintiff.

Appendices

GLOSSARY

Agency The fiduciary relationship that results from the manifestation of: (i) consent by one person to another that the other will act on his behalf and subject to his control; and (ii) the consent of the other to so act.[18]

Anchor investor Qualified institutional buyer in a public offer making an application for a value exceeding a certain threshold. concept of "anchor investor" in public issues in July 2009 with a view to create a significant impact on pricing of initial public offers. An anchor investor can attract investors to initial public offers because they infuse confidence in a security.

Arm's length transaction A transaction between either: (i) two unrelated and unaffiliated parties; or (ii) two related, affiliated parties, where measures are taken to prevent any potential conflicts of interest from arising.

Articles of incorporation The corporate charter that is filed with the state when registering a corporation.

Asset acquisition merger *See* TYPE C (INFORMAL OR PRACTICAL) ACQUISITION.

Balance sheet A statement of an entity's current financial data, including its assets, liabilities and owners' equity. It indicates the residual interest in assets of an entity after subtracting its liabilities.

Bridge loan Short-term loan typically taken out for a period of generally less than one year, allowing the borrower to meet current obligations pending the arrangement of larger, longer-term or permanent financing. *Also known as* "bridging loan" (UK) and "bridging finance" (South Africa).

Business judgment rule The doctrine that shields managers from liability when they exercise good faith business judgment based on a reasonable investigation when making a decision.

Business organization A legal entity through which investors and entrepreneurs provide goods and services and engage in trade and other wealth-generating activities.

C corporation A type of corporation recognized as a legal person whose profits are taxed under Subchapter C of the IRC. It is the default form that corporations take when registered. *Compare* S CORPORATION.

Close corporation *See* CLOSELY HELD CORPORATION.

Closely held corporation A corporation whose voting shares are owned by the directors and officers directly, rather than by shareholders in a publicly traded forum. The corporation is

---

[18] RLA § 1.

managed by the stockholders, not by a board of directors. In some states, there must be thirty-five or fewer officers to qualify as a closely held corporation. *Also termed* CLOSE CORPORATION.

Common stock Stock issued by a corporation that confers upon its holder the right to vote in corporate decisions and to receive dividends (after dividends have been paid out to holders of PREFERRED STOCK).

Open-ended investment company Company in which the money invested by savers is pooled and collectively invested in the markets by professional fund managers appointed by the company. The advantage to investors is that by putting their savings together with savings of other individuals, they get the benefits of diversification and of professional fund management. *Also known* as Investment company with variable capital.

Compound interest Interest calculated based on the aggregate sum of the principal plus any accrued interest. *See* SIMPLE INTEREST.

Conglomerate A large corporate entity that manages unrelated companies providing diverse goods and services (*e.g.*, textiles, medicine, media, etc.).

Corporate opportunity doctrine The rule that prohibits a corporation's directors, officers and employees from taking personal advantage of opportunities in which the corporation has a reasonable proprietary interest. An employee may not, for example, use his corporate position or information obtained from his official capacity to seize opportunities that by right belong to the corporation.

Debenture A long-term, unsecured debt issued by a corporation to generate capital. As an unsecured instrument, it is repaid only after secured debts have been liquidated.

Derivative Contract that derives its value from the performance of an underlying asset, index or interest rate. Derivatives can be used for a number of purposes, including insuring against price movements (hedging), increasing exposure to price movements for speculation or getting access to otherwise hard-to-trade assets or markets. Derivatives include forwards, futures, options, swaps, synthetic collateralized debt obligations and credit default swaps.

Derivative suit A lawsuit brought by shareholders on behalf of a corporation to enforce a right or correct a wrong. Recovery is made to the corporation, which is a party to the action.

Dissolution Formal, legal closure and termination of a business, normally preceded the LIQUIDATION of the Company's assets. The company articles of incorporation will lay out the process for corporate dissolution. *Compare* LIQUIDATION.

Efficient market hypothesis The theory that prices in financial markets reflect all available information at any time, since financial markets are "informationally efficient." The prices of traded assets are always therefore fairly based on the aggregate understanding of investors.

Equal dignity rule Whatever the means through which a merger is effected, the merger is valid as long as it follows the respective formalities, regardless of whether the shareholders would have gotten a better deal if the transaction had been cast in some other form.

Fiduciary duty The duty of care and duty of loyalty; duty to act with utmost honesty, putting the interests of others before one's own interests (example: the duty owed between partners).

Golden parachute Agreement between a company and an employee to remove the employee from the company in exchange for significant financial benefits (*e.g.*, compensating one of the presents of a company a significant bonus in exchange for the termination of the employment following a merger).

Hedge fund Investment vehicle and business structure that normally takes the form of a LP or LLC that is administered by a professional management firm to pool capital from a number of investors to invest in securities and other instruments. Hedge funds are generally distinct from private equity funds in that the majority of hedge funds invest in relatively liquid assets.

Income statement A financial summary of an entity's assets over a *period* structured as a statement of the entity's revenues (increases in equity) and expenses (decreases in equity).

Initial public offering ("IPO") The initial issuance of common or preferred stocks by a company to the public.

Insider trading Transactions in securities based on inside or advance information.

Internal affairs rule The rule representing the majority approach of most states whereby a corporation, regardless of where it operates or where its shareholders or assets are located, is bound by the law of the state of its incorporation, which will govern how the corporation is run.

Intra vires (Lat., "within the power") Within the scope of an individual's or corporation's power. *See* ULTRA VIRES.

Intrinsic fairness test A standard used to evaluate the allegation that a director or controlling shareholder engaged in an act of self-dealing. The standard requires the dominant shareholder or director to show that, although he (or it, in case the dominant shareholder is a corporation) engaged in self-dealing, the questioned transaction was fair to the corporation. *See* BUSINESS JUDGMENT RULE.

Joint and several liability Liability in which each member of a group is responsible for the full payment of a judgment, debt or other obligation of any other member of the group, leaving the members of the group to sort out the respective portions of the debt. *Compare* JOINT LIABILITY and SEVERAL LIABILITY.

Joint liability Liability of two or more persons (*e.g.*, spouses) for the full amount of a particular judgment, debt or other obligation. *Compare* SEVERAL LIABILITY and JOINT AND SEVERAL LIABILITY.

Joint venture Business arrangement between two or more persons, companies or a combination thereof that agree to pool together their resources for the purpose of accomplishing a specific task, to divide profits and share expenses and any potential losses.

Leveraged buyout Acquisition of a company using borrowed funds. Often, the assets of the target company or of the purchaser are used as collateral for the loans or other borrowed funds. Leveraged buyouts permit companies to make large acquisitions without committing significant sums of capital.

Leveraging A use of credit where an investor puts up a certain degree of an investment in equity and the rest on credit. As the return on the investment increases, the return on equity increases exponentially.

Liability An obligation or debt arising from a present duty to transfer assets to a specified third party because of past transactions or events.

Limited liability company A business entity that in many ways combines the advantages of the corporation with those of the partnership. Like the corporation, the LLC protects investors with limited liability equal to the amount they invest. Like a partnership, double taxation is avoided, since the investors, not the entity, are taxed directly.

Liquidation The conversion of a company's assets into cash through the sale of these company's assets, often undertaken when business closure is imminent. The cash is then used to pay off the company's debts and obligations. Liquidation need not be accompanied by a formal, legal DISSOLUTION of a company. *Compare* DISSOLUTION.

LLC *See* LIMITED LIABILITY COMPANY.

Loan-out corporation Typically used by athletes or entertainers, these corporations are formed to take in the individual's income, distribute certain fringe benefits such as health insurance or retirement funds and then to pay the athlete or entertainer the balance. This is done to avoid taxation on the fringe benefits.

Longstop date Last date by which a contractual condition or set of conditions must be satisfied or a duty must be performed.

Mezzanine financing Financing comprised of a combination of debt and equity that is generally used to finance the expansion of existing companies that permits the lender to convert the debt to an equity interest in the company if the debt is not paid back according to the terms of the loan.

National Association of Securities Dealers (NASD) "A group of brokers and dealers empowered by the SEC to regulate the over-the-counter securities market"[19]

National Association of Securities Dealers Automated Quotation System (NASDAQ) "A computerized system for recording transactions and displaying price quotations for a group of actively traded securities on the over-the-counter market."[20]

New York Stock Exchange (NYSE) An association handling the purchase and sale of securities. This is the dominant securities exchange in the United States. Companies traded on the NYSE are large companies having at least one million shares.

Owners' equity The owners' aggregate financial interests of an entity's *assets*, calculated as the amount by which an entity's *interest in assets* exceeds its *liabilities*. If an entity's total liabilities exceed its total assets, the owners' equity will be negative.

---

[19] Bryan A. Garner, ed., *Black's Law Dictionary*, "National Association of Securities Dealers" 1050 (8th ed. 2004).
[20] *Id.* "National Association of Securities Dealers Automated Quotation system" 1051.

Partnership An association of two or more partners (owners) to manage a business and share in control, profits and liability.

Pass-through taxation Taxation whereby only the owners of a business association, rather than the owners in addition to the business association, are taxed. Partnerships and S corporations enjoy pass-through taxation, as do LLCs that do not elect otherwise.

Piercing the corporate veil The act of imposing personal liability for a corporation's obligations on officers, directors or shareholders who are otherwise protected by limited liability.

Preemption Right *See* RIGHT OF FIRST REFUSAL.

Preferred stock Stock issued by a corporation that confers upon its holder priority over COMMON STOCK holders in the distribution of dividends, but that does not confer voting rights in corporate decision making.

Premium The sum above the nominal value of something, as in the premium price of stock where offerors make a *tender offer*: in exchange for an entire block of stock (thus transferring control of the corporation to the offeror), the offeree receives a premium above and beyond the market value of the stock.

Primary securities market The market that deals with securities that are issued by corporations to investors for the first time (as in the case of IPOs). *Compare* SECONDARY SECURITIES MARKET.

Private equity An asset class in finance consisting of equity securities and debt in operating companies that are not publicly traded on a stock exchange. Private equity provides working capital to a target company to nurture expansion, new-product development or restructuring of the company's operations, management or ownership.

Promoter An entrepreneur who identifies an opportunity and takes the initial steps in forming a business to capitalize on the opportunity, forming a corporation as the vehicle for investment. The promoter's fiduciary duty towards a corporation is similar to that owed by an agent to a principal.

Proxy contest A battle against a corporation's management mounted by a faction of dissatisfied shareholders that seek from uncommitted shareholders the right to vote their shares in favor of the faction's directors. *Also termed* PROXY FIGHT.

Proxy fight *See* PROXY CONTEST.

Redemption A corporation's repurchase of its securities from stockholders according to the terms of its securities agreement.

Revised Uniform Partnership Act (RUPA) A model statute that has been adopted by the majority of states and that aims to bring uniformity to state partnership statutes by revising the UPA of 1914. The term "Revised Uniform Partnership Act" generally refers to the 1994 revision, although it is also used to refer to other revisions, such as that of 1997.

Right of first refusal Contractual right to enter a business transaction with a second party according to specified terms, before the second party may enter into that transaction with a third party. Also known as PREEMPTION RIGHT.

Rule 144A Under Section 5 of the Securities Act, all offers and sales of securities must: (i) be registered with the SEC; or (ii) qualify for an exemption from the registration requirements. A party that wishes to publicly sell restricted or control securities may need to make special efforts to show that the sale is exempt from registration. Rule 144 provides an exemption and permits the public resale of restricted or control securities if a number of conditions are met, including how long the securities are held, the way in which they are sold and the amount that can be sold at any one time.

S corporation A type of corporation that permits the election for taxation under Subchapter S of the IRC, which exempts the organization from taxation, allowing gains and losses to instead be claimed on the individual tax returns of the corporation's owners. *Compare* C CORPORATION.

Secondary securities market The market where formerly issued securities are exchanged or traded, among investors via stock exchanges (such as the NASDAQ). *Compare* PRIMARY SECURITIES MARKET.

Securities Written certificates showing ownership of shares of stock, bonds or other interests involving an investment in an enterprise with the return dependent on the efforts of some third party, rather than on the direct participation of the investor in the enterprise.

Securities Act of 1933 A federal law that regulates the primary securities market, emphasizing public disclosure of all financial information and requiring that corporations, before making IPOs, file a *registration statement* with the SEC.

Securities and Exchange Commission ("SEC") A federal regulatory agency created by the SECURITIES EXCHANGE ACT OF 1934 for enforcing the Exchange Act by promulgating rules regarding the issuance and public trading of securities and investigating and prosecuting violations of the rules.

Securities Exchange Act of 1934 ("Exchange Act") A federal law dealing primarily with regulating the secondary securities market (the public trading of securities). The Exchange Act established the SECURITIES AND EXCHANGE COMMISSION, which enforces the Exchange Act by promulgating rules governing the trading of securities.

Settlement (of securities) Business process whereby securities or interests in securities are delivered, usually in simultaneous exchange for payment of money, to fulfill contractual obligations. A derivative instrument is physically settled if the underlier is physically delivered in exchange for a specified payment or, with cash settlement, if the derivative settles for an amount of money equal to what the derivative's market value would be at maturity if it were a physically settled derivative.

Several liability Liability of two or more persons for their own respective portions of a shared debt. *Compare* JOINT LIABILITY and JOINT AND SEVERAL LIABILITY.

Simple interest Interest calculated based only on the principal, without taking into account any accrued interest. *See* COMPOUND INTEREST.

Sole proprietorship A business fully owned by one person, the sole proprietor, who holds all of the business's liabilities and assets. Although the owner operates the business in his personal capacity, many other individuals may be involved as managers or employees.

Staggered board A board of directors whose members are elected on a staggered schedule, whereby only part of the board can change in any given election. Members cannot be removed absent the showing of cause and the board size cannot be increased.

Sui generis "Of its own class" (Lat.); different from all others.

Tag-along rights Contractual obligation that permits a minority shareholder to join the transaction and sell his or her minority stake in the company if a majority shareholder sells his or her stake.

Tender offer A public invitation regulated by state and federal law directed to all shareholders of a corporation to tender their shares to the offeror at a given premium in order for the offeror to obtain control of the corporation. Tender offers may be published in a newspaper or other public advertisement.

Triangular merger A merger generally effected when a large corporation seeks to merge with a closely held or other small corporation. In order to avoid a statutorily imposed shareholder vote and appraisal remedy, the large corporation will form a subsidiary that merges with the small corporation. The subsidiary votes through its only shareholder, the large corporation, which is bound by the decision of its board of directors.

Type A (statutory) merger A merger effected by two corporations in accordance with statutorily prescribed procedures. Generally, states impose a mandatory shareholder vote and appraisal remedy for dissatisfied shareholders.

Type B (informal or practical) merger A merger effected by a corporation by purchasing shares directly from a target corporation's shareholders. No involvement between the boards of the two corporations is necessary. Once the acquiring corporation obtains a controlling interest of the target corporation, the target corporation will become a subsidiary. The parent corporation may then enter into a short-form statutory merger with the subsidiary.

Type C (informal or practical) acquisition An operation whereby a large corporation acquires a small corporation's assets, avoiding the target corporation's unforeseen liabilities, in exchange for cash, securities or both, leaving the target corporation with nothing but a shell. Typically, the target corporation then dissolves itself and distributes the cash or securities to its shareholders.

Ultra vires (Lat., "Beyond the granted powers") Beyond the authority granted by a corporate charter or by law. An *ultra vires* act may be held to be unenforceable. *See* INTRA VIRES.

Underlier Value from which a derivative derives its value.

Uniform Partnership Act (UPA) Drafted by the National Conference of Commissioners on Uniform State Laws, this 1914 model statute aims to bring uniformity among state partnership statutes. It is enacted in all states, with the exception of Louisiana.

Venture capital Capital coming from wealthy individuals or pension funds managed by people who invest in a promising startup venture.

Voting by proxy Voting by authorizing a person to vote on a shareholder's shares.

CHARTS AND GRAPHS

CHOICE OF ENTITY MATRICES

Corporations

General Characteristics

C Corporation	A corporation that is taxed under the IRC.
	Corporations are C corporations by default. A corporation must seek to become an S corporation through the IRC.
	They do not allow for deductions for losses.
S Corporation	A corporation taxed through its shareholders, not through the corporation as a legal person.
	Under subchapter S of the IRC, a company must have a limited number of shareholders in order to qualify for this status.
	It allows for deductions for losses.
Closely Held Corporation	In closely held corporations, the managers and owners are the same group or the same person. Thus, a corporation is not the only entity that can be closely held. General partnerships, limited partnerships, LLCs, etc., can also be closely held.
	In Delaware, there must be no more than 30 shareholders in order to qualify as closely held.

Limited Liability

C Corporation	Obligations incurred by employees of C corporations are debts and obligations of the corporation, not of shareholders, employees or directors. As for shareholders, they risk the amount they invested.
	Obligations and torts of the directors and officers belong to the corporation, not to the directors and officers personally, unless the corporate veil is pierced.

Control

C Corporation	Except for electing the board members, the owners (shareholders) usually do not control the corporation.
S Corporation	The owners are generally in control.
Closely Held Corporation	Involves few owners who usually are closely involved in management and who usually depend on the corporation for their livelihood.

Taxes

Business Organizations

C Corporation	The corporation is taxed.
	It is easier for corporations than for partnerships to make IRS deductions.
S Corporation	The corporation is not taxed; there is pass-through taxation, where the shareholders, not the corporation, are taxed.
Closely Held Corporation	Most closely held corporations are eligible to be treated as S corporations for tax purposes. In such cases, there is pass-through taxation, where the shareholders, not the corporation, are taxed.

Obligations and Duties

C Corporation	The management owes a duty of care and a duty of loyalty to the owners of the corporation that prohibits self-dealing, the seizure of corporate opportunity.
	The duties vary from state to state and are defined by the courts.
Closely Held Corporation	This area of the law is still developing and the fiduciary duties have not yet been fully defined.
	However, since closely held corporations have limited liquidity and pose an exit problem, many courts have imposed broader fiduciary duties on the management of closely held corporations than on the management of public corporations. The fiduciary duties of the management of closely held corporations are therefore broader than those owed by the directors and officers of C corporations.
	The duties are in many ways akin to the stricter duties imposed in the partnership model.

Flexibility and Scope

C Corporation	The corporation may be engaged in any lawful activities in accordance with the corporation's bylaws and articles of incorporation.
	The term is generally unlimited.
S Corporation	An S corporation generally has less formalities than a C corporation.
Closely Held Corporation	Since the owners manage the corporation, there is less formality and more flexibility (e.g., there is no board of directors, etc.).

Dissolution and Exit Ability

| C Corporation | Shareholders may easily transfer their ownership, since their shares are usually traded on public markets. |
| Closely Held Corporation | Because there is no public market for their shares, transferring ownership may be difficult. These are not easily liquidated. |

Partnerships

General Characteristics

Charts and Graphs

General Partnership	This is a voluntary agreement between two or more partners in which all participate in the management of a business for profit and all owe liability jointly and severally. The partners divide profits and losses among each other and their contributions may not be equal.
Limited Partnership (LP)	This is a business venture composed of at least one general partner who manages the affairs of the business and at least one limited partner who contributes capital and shares profits, but who may not manage the business.
Limited Liability Partnership (LLP)	This is a partnership in which none of the partners is liable for the negligent acts of any other partner or any employee not under his direct supervision. These are creatures of statute recognized in all States.
Limited Liability Limited Partnership	This is a type of limited partnership in which the general partner may also limit liability. These are seldom used today, since a general partner will generally incorporate if allowed by state law, thus obtaining limited liability protection.

Limited Liability

General Partnership	General partners have unlimited liability for the debts of the partnership. The liability is joint and several.
Limited Partnership (LP)	The general partner(s) have unlimited personal, joint and several liability; the limited partners are liable only for the amount they contributed, unless they cross a threshold of control, taking on the role of management.
Limited Liability Partnership (LLP)	Unlike in a general partnership, the personal liability of a partner in an LLP is limited to her own negligence or wrongdoing or that of any employee under the partner's supervision.
Limited Liability Limited Partnership	Both the limited and general partners are protected by limited liability.

Control

General Partnership	General partners have direct control. By default, the partners all have equal voices in management, but the control is flexible (*e.g.*, the partners may agree to delegate decision making authority or 51% control to one partner).
Limited Partnership (LP)	The general partners have full control and authority over management of the business. The limited partners resemble shareholders of a corporation: they are passive investors. However, limited partners may be given greater rights through the LP's organizational documents.
Limited Liability Partnership (LLP)	The partners are generally in control.
Limited Liability	As in an LP, the general partners have control of the partnership, while the limited partners do not.

Limited Partnership	The major difference is that while the general partners in a LP have unlimited liability, in an LLLP, their liability is limited to their investment.

Taxes

General Partnership	**Pass-through taxation** General partnerships are not taxed; the partners must report gains and losses on their individual tax returns.
Limited Partnership (LP)	**Pass-through taxation** The partners, not the corporation, are taxed.
Limited Liability Partnership (LLP)	**Pass-through taxation** The partners, not the corporation, are taxed.
Limited Liability Limited Partnership	**Pass-through taxation** The partners, not the corporation, are taxed.

Obligations and duties

General Partnership	The partners owe one another broad fiduciary duties that are wider in scope than those owed by corporate management to the corporation. It is the duty of utmost good faith and loyalty that prohibits self-dealing, seizing partnership opportunities and competing with the partnership. The duties may not be waived by contract.
Limited Partnership (LP)	The general partners owe all of the partners a duty of loyalty and fair dealing similar to that in general partnerships.
Limited Liability Partnership (LLP)	The partners owe one another a duty of loyalty and fair dealing similar to that in general partnerships.
Limited Liability Limited Partnership	The partners owe one another a duty of loyalty and fair dealing similar to that in general partnerships.

Flexibility and Scope

General Partnership	General partnerships offer more flexibility than corporations.
Limited Partnership (LP)	These offer more flexibility than corporations, but are limited in time and scope.

Limited Liability Partnership (LLP)	These offer more flexibility than corporations.
Limited Liability Limited Partnership	These offer more flexibility than corporations.

Dissolution and Exit Ability

General Partnership	Partnerships are usually designed to terminate at the death of the partners.
	If a partner decides to leave, the default rule requires that the entire partnership be disbanded (thereby requiring the sale of all assets to ensure that each partner received his fair share).

Sole Proprietorships, Joint Ventures, LLCs

General Characteristics

Sole Proprietorship	This is a business run by one person who owns all of the assets and owes all of the liabilities.
	Example: setting up and selling beverages at a lemonade stand.
Joint ventures	This is an association of two or more investors engaging in a commercial enterprise to gain a profit by pooling together their skills and resources.
	Elements:
	1. an express or implied agreement;
	2. a common purpose;
	3. shared profits and losses;
	4. equal voice among members.
	These are very similar to partnerships.
Limited Liability Company (LLC)	These companies are in many ways similar to partnerships, except that they are characterized by limited liability. They are authorized by statute in every state.
	They are small-business organizations whose investors are known as "members."
	Closely held firms may organize as LLCs. In addition, public firms may be able to register as an LLC, but would still be double-taxed.

Limited Liability

Sole Proprietorship	There is no legal separation between the person operating the business and the business itself. The two are one. Thus, the sole proprietor has unlimited liability for the business's obligations.
Joint ventures	These are fixed by agreement.
Limited Liability Company (LLC)	Unlike a partnership, an LLC is a legal person separate from its members that contracts its own debts, obligations and liabilities. LLC state statutes generally provide that neither the members nor the managers of LLCs are liable under judgment, decree or order of a

	court, or otherwise, for these debts, obligations and liabilities. LLCs thus offer their members an "LLC veil," similar to the "corporate veil" of corporations.
	Case law to date suggests that the LLC veil may, however, be pierced, giving rise to the personal liability of the LLC's members, in the same way that the corporate veil is pierced in the case of corporations—whenever company formalities are not respected and a fraud, injustice or inequity is furthered.
	Unlike in limited partnerships, the liability of an LLC member does not disappear because of his active participation in management.

Control

Sole Proprietorship	The sole proprietor retains full control, although he may mete out responsibilities to managers and other employees.
Joint ventures	By default, the joint venturers have equal voices in decision making. However, this may be altered by agreement.
Limited Liability Company (LLC)	Control is determined by an agreement that is usually called the "operating agreement." LLCs are generally managed by "members" or "managers."
	Unlike in a limited partnership, all of the managers of an LLC may participate in management without abrogating their limited liability.

Taxes

Sole Proprietorship	The sole proprietor is taxed directly; there is no legal entity that is taxed.
Limited Liability Company (LLC)	Like a partnership, an LLC has pass-through taxation and thereby avoids the double-taxation.
	However, if an LLC is public (as opposed to closely held), it loses the pass-through taxation benefit and is taxed the same way as a C corporation.

Obligations and duties

Sole Proprietorship	Inapplicable, since the sole proprietor is led by one person who owes no fiduciary duties to other owners.
Joint ventures	The fiduciary duties owed between co-venturers are similar to those owed by partners to one another. It is a strict duty of utmost loyalty and good faith.
Limited Liability Company (LLC)	This area of the law is still being developed and the scope of fiduciary duties owed by members of an LLC to one another is as of yet unclear. However, the duties may be eliminated in the operating agreement.

Flexibility and Scope

Sole Proprietorship	The sole proprietor has the flexibility to operate his business in any way permitted by the law.
Joint ventures	Joint ventures are created with limited scope.
Limited Liability	LLCs are intended to be more flexible than corporations. State law may require certain minimum formalities with which an LLC in that state must comply.

Company (LLC)	

Dissolution and Exit Ability

Sole Proprietorship	The sole proprietorship ends when the sole proprietor ceases doing business.
Joint ventures	These are of limited duration.
Limited Liability Company (LLC)	When an LLC is formed, a limited term of existence generally must be stated. In some states, the term must be no more than thirty years.
	Members may transfer their financial interest in the LLC. However, they may not transfer their management interest unless the other members unanimously consent or there is an agreement to the contrary.
	However, the members may withdraw at will. Usually, they may do so with notice of six months.

TABLE OF CASES

Table of Cases

www.ingramcontent.com/pod-product-compliance
Lightning Source LLC
Chambersburg PA
CBHW081508200326
41518CB00015B/2431